THE VITALITY OF THE INDIVIDUAL IN THE THOUGHT OF ANCIENT ISRAEL

By

AUBREY R. JOHNSON

CARDIFF
UNIVERSITY OF WALES PRESS
1964

FIRST EDITION 1949
SECOND EDITION 1964

194382

PRINTED IN GREAT BRITAIN

TO THE MEMORY OF

ANN ELIZABETH HALL

A DEAR FRIEND OF THE FAMILY

THROUGH THREE GENERATIONS

PREFACE

THE ensuing study is of a preliminary character, being the first of a series of monographs designed to elucidate the famous saying of Habakkuk (ii. 4b): וְצַדִּיק בֶּאֱמוּנָתוֹ יִחְיֶה. This, as it seems to me, formulates a principle which in one way or another runs like a thread through the whole of the Old as well as the New Testament, and so is of fundamental importance for the fashioning of a sound Biblical Theology.

Accordingly the following pages should not be regarded as in any way representing an attempt to furnish a comprehensive picture of the Israelite conception of man. Indeed one should not fail to ask the question as to how far we may be justified in holding that there was, as a matter of fact, anything like a uniform conception. Nevertheless, as the Israelite appears to have shown little interest in speculative thinking, it does seem possible to take a broad general treatment of this kind as being fairly representative. At the same time I have tried constantly to bear in mind the possible existence of different levels of thought, the more so as there seems to be a real danger in Old Testament study as a whole of misinterpreting what may be different but contemporary *strata* in terms of corresponding *stages* of thought, which can be arranged chronologically so as to fit into an over-simplified evolutionary scheme or similar theory of progressive revelation.

Further, my employment of the familiar symbols J, E, D, H, and P should not be construed as indicating a complete acceptance of the documentary theories usually associated with them, although I have yet to be convinced that some such analysis (with the possible exception of E or much of E) is not required by the facts. It should certainly not be held to imply an acceptance of the normal attempt to present the religion of Israel in its historical development which is now commonly associated with the name of Wellhausen.

If an apology be required for the fullness of the notes, which may well seem burdensome to many readers, it must be that these are intended as much for my own future use as for anyone who may wish to examine the evidence for my statements or even pursue a similar line of inquiry for himself. The fact is that the monographs referred to are also designed as prolegomena to something like a Biblical Theology; and this, if it is to be done properly, must proceed from a searching analysis of all the data and a willingness to use every philological aid at one's disposal. Having made this ambitious claim, however, I must add that no one can be better aware than I of how far short I come of attaining this ideal; I can only say that I have done my best amid the many demands made upon my time by my ordinary professional duties.

I take this opportunity of acknowledging the generous help which I have received from Professor O. Eissfeldt, who was kind enough to furnish me with certain German material which would not otherwise have been available, and Professors S. A. Cook and G. R. Driver, and the Rev. Professors N. W. Porteous, T. H. Robinson, and H. H. Rowley, each of whom has kindly read through the whole of the typescript and given freely of his own expert knowledge and criticism. I am also greatly indebted to the Rev. Professor G. H. Davies, not only for similar kindness, but also for his assistance in reading the proofs.

Finally, I should like to express my warm thanks to the University of Wales Press for again accepting my work for publication, and to the Oxford University Press for the characteristic skill and care bestowed upon it, not only in this instance, but also on previous occasions.

AUBREY R. JOHNSON

Cardiff
March 1949

PREFACE TO THE SECOND EDITION

IN preparing this edition I have revised the work throughout. While I have found little reason to make changes in the text, the footnotes have been enlarged and brought, I hope, reasonably up to date, and a set of indexes has been supplied in conformity with the other volumes in the series. In this connexion I recall that, when the first edition was published, some of my friends complained that it would have been the better for an index; I now confidently await the complaint that one may have too much of a good thing!

I am glad to take this opportunity of thanking Mr. C. R. Busby, of Messrs. Burns & Oates Ltd., for his kindness in lending me a file copy of the second edition of the late Father Sutcliffe's book, *The Old Testament and the Future Life*, which was unfortunately out of print and not readily accessible just when I needed it.

As the type has been completely reset for this edition, I must give expression once again to the deep sense of obligation which I feel towards the Oxford University Press for the care with which the book has been produced. Warm thanks are also due to my colleagues and friends, the Rev. E. R. Rowlands and the Rev. C. G. Williams, who generously gave up much valuable time in order to help with the task of checking the typescript and reading the proofs.

AUBREY R. JOHNSON

Cardiff
March 1964

PRINCIPAL ABBREVIATIONS

A.A.S.F.	Annales Academiæ Scientiarum Fennicæ.
A.J.S.L.	*American Journal of Semitic Languages and Literatures.*
A.T.D.	Das Alte Testament Deutsch.
B.A.S.O.R.	*Bulletin of the American Schools of Oriental Research.*
B.D.B.	Brown, Driver, and Briggs, *A Hebrew and English Lexicon of the Old Testament* (1906), corrected impression (1952).
B.O.	*Bibliotheca Orientalis.*
B.Q.	*The Baptist Quarterly.*
B.T.L.V.N.I.	*Bijdragen tot de taal-, land- en volkenkunde van Nederlandsch-Indië.*
B.V.S.A.W.L.	Berichte über die Verhandlungen der sächsischen Akademie der Wissenschaften zu Leipzig. Phil.-hist. Klasse.
B.W.A.N.T.	Beiträge zur Wissenschaft vom Alten und Neuen Testament.
B.Z.A.W.	Beihefte zur *Zeitschrift für die alttestamentliche Wissenschaft.*
C.A.H.	*The Cambridge Ancient History.*
C.B.	Cambridge Bible.
C.B.Q.	*The Catholic Biblical Quarterly.*
Cent.B.	The Century Bible.
C.T.	Cahiers théologiques.
C.W.	*Christentum und Wissenschaft.*
D	The Deuteronomic narrative (*or* code), or the Deuteronomic school.
D.B.	*A Dictionary of the Bible*, ed. J. Hastings (1898–1904).
E	The Elohistic narrative (*or* code), or the Elohist.
E.B.	Études Bibliques.
Echt.B.	Echter Bibel.
E.H.P.R.	Études d'histoire et de philosophie religieuses.
E.T.	*The Expository Times.*
G.K.	Gesenius–Kautzsch, *Hebrew Grammar*, 2nd English edition, rev. by A. E. Cowley (1910).
H	The Holiness code.
H.A.T.	Handbuch zum Alten Testament.
H.K.	Handkommentar zum Alten Testament.
H.S.A.T.	Die Heilige Schrift des Alten Testamentes (Bonner Bibel).
H.S.A.T.	E. Kautzsch (ed.), *Die Heilige Schrift des Alten Testaments*, 4th edition, ed. A. Bertholet (1922–3).
H.U.C.A.	*Hebrew Union College Annual.*
I.B.	The Interpreter's Bible.
I.C.C.	The International Critical Commentary.
J	The Yahwistic narrative (*or* code), or the Yahwist.

J.B.L.	*Journal of Biblical Literature.*
J.Q.R.	*Jewish Quarterly Review.*
J.R.A.S.	*Journal of the Royal Asiatic Society.*
J.S.S.	*Journal of Semitic Studies.*
J.T.S.	*The Journal of Theological Studies.*
K.A.T.	Kommentar zum Alten Testament.
K.B.	L. Koehler and W. Baumgartner, *Lexicon in Veteris Testamenti Libros* (1953), including *Supplementum ad Lexicon in Veteris Testamenti Libros* (1958).
K.e.H.	Kurzgefasstes exegetisches Handbuch zum Alten Testament.
K.H.C.	Kurzer Hand-Commentar zum Alten Testament.
L	Old Latin Version.
LXX	The Septuagint.
M.T.	The Massoretic Text.
N.A.W.G.	Nachrichten der Akademie der Wissenschaften in Göttingen, I. Phil.-hist. Klasse.
N.H.	New (Late) Hebrew.
Nor.T.T.	*Norsk Teologisk Tidsskrift.*
O.T.S.	Old Testament Studies.
O.T.S.	*Oudtestamentische Studiën.*
P	The Priestly narrative (*or* code), or the Priestly school.
P.E.Q.	*Palestine Exploration Quarterly.*
R.B.	*Revue Biblique.*
R.E.S.	*Revue des études sémitiques et Babyloniaca.*
R.H.R.	*Revue de l'histoire des religions.*
R.P.	*Revue philosophique de la France et de l'Étranger.*
S	The Syriac Version (Peshiṭta).
S.B.	La Sainte Bible, texte latin et traduction française d'après les textes originaux avec un commentaire exégétique et théologique.
S.B.J.	La Sainte Bible traduite en français sous la direction de l'École Biblique de Jérusalem.
S.E.Å.	*Svensk Exegetisk Årsbok.*
S.G.V.S.	Sammlung gemeinverständlicher Vorträge und Schriften aus dem Gebiet der Theologie und Religionsgeschichte.
S.O.	Studia Orientalia edidit Societas Orientalis Fennica.
S.V.T.	Supplements to *Vetus Testamentum.*
T	Targum.
T.R.	*Theologische Rundschau.*
T.S.K.	*Theologische Studien und Kritiken.*
Th.W.N.T.	*Theologisches Wörterbuch zum Neuen Testament*, ed. G. Kittel and G. Friedrich (1933–).
T.Z.	*Theologische Zeitschrift.*
V	The Vulgate.
V.K.A.W.A.	Verhandelingen der Koninklijke Akademie van Wetenschappen te Amsterdam. Afdeeling Letterkunde.

V.T.	Vetus Testamentum.
W.C.	Westminster Commentaries.
W.O.	Die Welt des Orients.
Z.A.W.	Zeitschrift für die alttestamentliche Wissenschaft.
Z.M.R.	Zeitschrift für Missionskunde und Religionswissenschaft.
Z.T.K.	Zeitschrift für Theologie und Kirche.

THE VITALITY OF THE INDIVIDUAL
IN THE THOUGHT OF ANCIENT
ISRAEL

I

ANY attempt at a successful interpretation of the Bible
seems bound to take note of the fact that Israelite thinking,
like that of the so-called 'primitive' peoples of the present
day,[1] is predominantly synthetic.[2] It is characterized in large
measure by what has been called the grasping of a totality.[3]
Phenomena are readily perceived as being in some kind of
relationship; they are readily found to participate in some
sort of whole.[4] This recognition of the mental activity of

---

[1] Cf., for example, L. Lévy-Bruhl, *Les Fonctions mentales dans les sociétés
inférieures* (1910), E.T. by L. A. Clare, *How Natives Think* (1926); *La
Mentalité primitive* (1922), E.T. by L. A. Clare, *Primitive Mentality* (1923);
G. van der Leeuw, *La Structure de la mentalité primitive* (1928). For a
criticism of this use of the term 'primitive', see O. Leroy, *La Raison primitive:
Essai de réfutation de la théorie du prélogisme* (1927), pp. 16 f.; S. H. Hooke
(editor), *Myth and Ritual: Essays on the Myth and Ritual of the Hebrews in
relation to the Culture Pattern of the Ancient East* (1933), pp. 1 f.; and so
often. Cf. E. Westermarck, *The Origin and Development of the Moral Ideas*,
i, 2nd edit. (1912), p. 25.

[2] Cf. J. Koeberle, *Natur und Geist nach der Auffassung des Alten Testa-
ments* (1901), pp. 76 ff.; S. A. Cook, in *C.A.H.* i, 2nd edit. (1924), pp. 195 ff.,
The Old Testament: A Reinterpretation (1936), pp. 107 ff.; J. Pedersen, *Israel
I–II: Sjæleliv og Samfundsliv* (1920), 2nd edit. rev. (1933), 3rd edit. (1958),
E.T., *Israel: its Life and Culture I–II* (1926), 2nd edit. (1959), as cited below.

[3] Pedersen, op. cit., pp. 80–101, E.T., pp. 106–33. This valuable work
(like its sequel, *Israel III–IV: Hellighed og Guddommelighed* (1934), 2nd edit.
rev. (1960), E.T., *Israel: its Life and Culture III–IV* (1940), 2nd edit. with
additions (1959)) should be in the hands of every student of the Old Testament, but it must be used critically and with caution. Cf., for example, G.
Hölscher, in *T.S.K.* (1937–8), pp. 234–62; and see below, p. 2, n. 2, p. 3,
n. 4.

[4] To avoid such a misunderstanding as that of N. H. Snaith, *J.T.S.* xliv
(1943), pp. 81–84, in a review of the writer's monograph, *The One and the
Many in the Israelite Conception of God* (1942), it may be pointed out that
the adoption of an element in Lévy-Bruhl's terminology should not be held
to imply an acceptance of his associated theories, especially that of a 'prelogical' mentality or even that of a *law* of 'participation'. For a criticism of

the Israelites as predominantly synthetic, the awareness of totality, is important.[1] It is, perhaps, hardly too much to say that it is the 'Open Sesame' which unlocks the secrets of the Hebrew language and reveals the riches of the Israelite mind.[2]

Thus one finds that it is this awareness of a totality which governs what is apparently the normal conception of man both in the thinking of the above-mentioned 'primitive' peoples and in that of the Israelites. In the former case man is commonly thought of as a unit of vital power, i.e. 'soul-stuff' or 'soul-substance' (*zielestof*), as it has been called.[3] He is seen to form a psychical whole. Moreover, this soul-stuff or soul-substance is perceived, not only in the various members

Lévy-Bruhl's views, see Leroy, op. cit., *passim*; P. Radin, *Primitive Man as a Philosopher* (1927), pp. 27 ff., 229 ff.; and so often. Indeed, see now Lévy-Bruhl's partial renunciation of his theories as recorded in 'Les "Carnets" de Lucien Lévy-Bruhl', *R.P.* cxxxvii (1947), pp. 257–81.

[1] T. Boman, *Das hebräische Denken im Vergleich mit dem Griechischen*, 3rd edit. rev. (1959), p. 194, n. 292, E.T. by J. L. Moreau, *Hebrew Thought compared with Greek* (1960), p. 202, n. 3, claims that, when I thus describe Israelite thinking as 'synthetic', I really mean 'ganzheitlich' ('holistic'); but the fact is that I mean just what I say, and my language was carefully chosen in order to indicate that I was avoiding the kind of approach subsequently made by Boman, which seems to me to be without foundation. Indeed, while thus retaining my expression 'predominantly synthetic', I should like to stress the adverb 'predominantly', which was intended from the first as a safeguard against appearing to overlook the analytical aspects of Israelite thinking. Cf. the warning in the preceding note which, in the circumstances, I have expanded slightly for this edition.

[2] Cf. Pedersen, *Israel I–II*, pp. 80 ff., E.T., pp. 106 ff.; T. H. Robinson, *The Genius of Hebrew Grammar* (1928), *passim*. Here again, however, caution is necessary: cf. J. Barr, *The Semantics of Biblical Language* (1961), pp. 89 ff.; and see above, p. 1, n. 3.

[3] For this somewhat ugly but (within limits) useful expression, as employed originally by A. C. Kruyt, *Het animisme in den Indischen Archipel* (1906), see the works of Lévy-Bruhl and van der Leeuw which are cited below; also, for example, W. H. R. Rivers, 'The Concept of "Soul-Substance" in New Guinea and Melanesia', in *Psychology and Ethnology* (1926), pp. 97–119. For Kruyt's own comments on its limitations, see his article, 'Measa, eene bijdrage tot (de kennis van) het dynamisme der Bare'e-sprekende Toradja's en enkele omwonende volken', *B.T.L.V.N.I.* lxxiv (1918), pp. 233–60, lxxv (1919), pp. 36–133, lxxvi (1920), pp. 1–116; but a more serious limitation, as it seems to me, is the fact that it serves to encourage what appears to be a question-begging use of the term 'soul' (and its parallels) in contexts of the kind noted below, p. 3, n. 4.

and secretions of the body, but also in a more extended form in whatever bears traces of contact with him. This class may include former secretions such as blood, spittle, and sweat; the shadow, reflection, and similar reproductions; footprints and other bodily impressions; or, again, personal possessions such as wearing apparel, weapons, and domestic utensils: and, finally, coupled with these there are those vaguer conceptions known as the 'dream-soul', the 'bird-soul', the 'external soul', and the like.[1] A potential unity is thought to exist between the whole and any such part, however separate the latter may appear to a more analytical type of mind: and this is the principle which lies behind the practice of what has been called 'contagious magic'.[2] Accordingly, for the so-called 'primitive', a man's individuality does not stop short at his bodily exterior; he is conscious of a very lively 'extension of the personality'.[3]

Now the Israelite conception of man, if it is to be understood, must be seen in this light, for similar ideas are often latent and sometimes clearly expressed in the literature of the Old Testament. The place of honour in this connexion (as in any discussion of the Israelite conception of man) must go, of course, to the somewhat elusive term נֶפֶשׁ, which admits a remarkably wide range of meaning.[4] Indeed

---

[1] Cf. J. G. Frazer, *The Golden Bough*, 3rd edit. (1911–15), *passim*; L. Lévy-Bruhl, *L'Âme primitive* (1927), E.T. by L. A. Clare, *The 'Soul' of the Primitive* (1928), Introduction and Chapters iii–iv; G. van der Leeuw, *Phäno-menologie der Religion* (1933), pp. 254 ff., 2nd edit. rev. (1956), pp. 311 ff., E.T. by J. E. Turner, *Religion in Essence and Manifestation* (1938), pp. 275 ff.

[2] i.e. by Frazer, who draws a distinction between (*a*) homoeopathic or imitative magic, based upon the principle that 'like produces like', and (*b*) contagious magic, based upon the principle that 'things which have once been in contact with each other continue to act on each other at a distance after the physical contact has been severed'. Op. cit., I. i, p. 52. See also A. Bertholet, *Das Dynamistische im Alten Testament*, S.G.V.S. 121 (1926), pp. 36 f.

[3] For this expressive phrase, adopted by Lévy-Bruhl, op. cit., p. 142, E.T., pp. 121 f., see J. van Wing, *Études Bakongo* (1920), p. 129. Cf. *The One and the Many in the Israelite Conception of God*, pp. 6 ff., 2nd edit. (1961), pp. 2 ff.: and see again p. 1, n. 4.

[4] The most recent study of this term known to the writer, when the first edition of this monograph was published, was that of J. H. Becker, *Het begrip nefesj in het Oude Testament* (1942), which may be cordially recommended

4　　The Vitality of the Individual

there is some slight justification for noting even at this point the cardinal fact, to which repeated reference will be made, that in Israelite thought psychical functions have close physical associations;[1] for there is reason to believe that נֶפֶשׁ, like the cognate Accadian NAPIŠTU and the Ugaritic *npš*, was used *inter alia* to denote the 'throat' or 'neck',[2]

on the whole for its clear marshalling of the data and its useful bibliography. This may now be supplemented by A. Murtonen, *The Living Soul: A Study of the Meaning of the word* næfæš *in the Old Testament Hebrew Language*, S.O. xxiii. 1 (1958); and D. Lys, *Nèphèsh: Histoire de l'âme dans la révélation d'Israël au sein des religions proche-orientales*, E.H.P.R. 50 (1959), coupled with the short but discerning review of this work by A. Guillaumont, in *R.H.R.* clxi (1962), pp. 247 f. Cf., too, G. Pidoux, *L'Homme dans l'Ancien Testament*, C.T. 32 (1953), pp. 10 ff. Each of these special studies may be read with profit; but unfortunately, like the pioneer work of Pedersen (e.g. *Israel I–II*, pp. 73 ff., E.T., pp. 97 ff.), they are marred for the present writer by what seems to be a questionable use of the term 'soul' (*sjæl, âme*) which, in Pedersen's case, was apparently encouraged by the otherwise valuable and stimulating work of V. Grønbech, *Vor Folkeæt i Oldtiden* (1909–12), E.T. by W. Worster (revised and in part rewritten by the author), *The Culture of the Teutons* (1931), 2nd Danish edition, revised and enlarged along the lines of the English edition (1955): cf., too, what Grønbech has to say in 'Soul or Mana?', *Actes du IVe congrès international d'histoire des religions* (1913), pp. 69 f., and 'Primitiv Religion', in *Illustreret Religionshistorie*, ed. J. Pedersen (1948), pp. 11–73. Finally it may be pointed out that the ensuing discussion of the term נֶפֶשׁ is based upon an independent examination of all the examples of its use which are to be found in the Old Testament (excluding, at this stage, the Apocrypha); and this statement applies *mutatis mutandis* to all the other terms which are discussed in the following pages.

[1] Cf. Koeberle, op. cit., pp. 178–228; H. W. Robinson, *The Christian Doctrine of Man*, 3rd edit. (1926), pp. 11–27; 'Hebrew Psychology', in *The People and the Book*, ed. A. S. Peake (1925), pp. 353 ff.; P. (E.) Dhorme, 'L'Emploi métaphorique des noms de parties du corps en hébreu et en accadien', *R.B.* xxix (1920), pp. 465–506; xxx (1921), pp. 374–99, 517–40; xxxi (1922), pp. 215–33, 489–517; xxxii (1923), pp. 185–212; reproduced in book form in 1923; Pedersen, op. cit., *passim*; S. A. Cook, in his notes to W. R. Smith, *The Religion of the Semites*, 3rd edit. (1927), pp. 634 f.; W. Eichrodt, *Theologie des Alten Testaments*, ii (1935), pp. 65–77, ii–iii, 4th edit. rev. (1961), pp. 84–99.

[2] Cf. Dhorme, op. cit., pp. 18 f.; L. Dürr, in *Z.A.W.* xliii (1925), pp. 262 ff.; also J. Weill, *Z.A.W.* xliv (1926), pp. 62 f.; F. Rüsche, *Blut, Leben und Seele* (1930), pp. 311 ff. and (with caution) pp. 336 ff.; G. R. Driver, in *W.O.* (1948), pp. 237 f. For the Ugaritic *npš* in this sense, see W. F. Albright, in *B.A.S.O.R.* 83 (Oct. 1941), p. 41 (as cited again below, p. 5, n. 3). Note, however, that C. F. Jean, in *Mélanges syriens offerts à Monsieur René Dussaud*, ii (1939), pp. 708–12, while recognizing this meaning of the term,

i.e. as the organ through which one breathed.[1] Thus Isaiah apparently used it in this sense when, in denouncing the Jerusalem of his day,[2] he described its ultimate fate as follows:[3]

> Therefore
> Sheol hath widened its throat (נֶפֶשׁ),
> And opened its mouth without limit;
> And down goeth her pride, her clamour,
> Her tumult, every jubilant one within her!

Similarly the author of the psalm ascribed to Jonah, in using a common metaphor to illustrate the deep distress from which he has been delivered by Yahweh, thus describes the way in which he was being sucked down through the waters of the great cosmic sea to the lasting abode of the dead:[4]

inclines to the view that it originally denoted 'blood', a significance which would have a parallel in the cognate Arabic term نَفْس; but in the present writer's opinion Jean's whole treatment of this term (both here and in 'Tentatives d'explication du "moi" chez les anciens peuples de l'Orient méditerranéen', *R.H.R.* cxxi (1940), pp. 109–27) needs to be read with the utmost caution. The same must be said of R. Dussaud, 'La Notion d'âme chez les Israélites et les Phéniciens', *Syria* xvi (1935), pp. 267–77 (cf. *Les Origines cananéennes du sacrifice israélite*, 2nd edit. (1941), pp. 83–85); 'La néphesh et la rouaḥ dans le "Livre de Job" ', *R.H.R.* cxxix (1945), pp. 17–30; and A. Heidel, *The Gilgamesh Epic and Old Testament Parallels* (1946), pp. 143 ff.

[1] See below, p. 6, n. 1.

[2] This is the probable reference (cf., for example, G. B. Gray, I.C.C. (1912), O. Procksch, K.A.T. (1930), J. Fischer, H.S.A.T. (1937), *in loc.*); but it is also conceivable that the prophet had in mind the country as a whole (cf., for example, O. Kaiser, A.T.D. (1960), but not 2nd edit. (1963), *in loc.*).

[3] v. 14. Cf. the similar use in Hab. ii. 5, and the still more striking parallel in Ugaritic which is reproduced by Albright, loc. cit. (= C. H. Gordon, *Ugaritic Manual* (1955), ii, 67 I, 6–8; G. R. Driver, *Canaanite Myths and Legends*, O.T.S. 3 (1956), B I* i 6–8). On the other hand, Prov. xxviii. 25 is less convincing; and, while the parallelism with 'mouth' appears to offer clear confirmation in the case of the passage quoted, the present writer cannot agree that this is so as regards the parallelism in Pss. xliv. 26 (EVV. 25) (cf. Ps. cxix. 25), lxiii. 6 (EVV. 5), Prov. iii. 22, and Eccles. vi. 7 (similarly Isa. li. 23).

[4] Jonah ii. 6 f. (EVV. 5 f.), as below, pp. 90 ff. Cf. the close parallel in Ps. lxix. 2 (EVV. 1); and for fuller treatment of this important simile, see below, loc. cit. On the other hand, again, it is difficult to be convinced that a similar interpretation is warranted in the case of Ps. cxxiv. 4, 5 (עַל־נַפְשֵׁנוּ bis). In fact, most of the remaining examples suggested by Dürr seem extremely

Water encompassed me up to the neck (עַד־נֶפֶשׁ);
The deep surrounded me.
Reeds became entwined about my head
    At the bases of the mountains.
I went down to the land whose bars
    Were to be about me for ever.

A corresponding use of the term נֶפֶשׁ to denote 'breath'
may be readily understood,[1] even though there be no certain
example of its use in this way.[2] Indeed there is something

doubtful; and, despite the considerable support which he now receives from
K.B., s.v., it is unlikely that the meaning 'throat' or 'neck' is to be found in
more than ten or a dozen passages at most, including, in addition to the four
already cited, Job xli. 13 (EVV. 21), as reproduced below, n. 2; Ps. cv. 18
(*pace* J. Brinktrine, in *Z.A.W.* lxiv (1952), pp. 251–8); Prov. xxiii. 7a (cf.
Weill, loc. cit.), xxviii. 25 (i.e. 'broad of throat' = 'voracious', 'greedy': cf.
Isa. v. 14, Hab. ii. 5, as cited in the preceding note).

[1] It seems quite clear that נֶפֶשׁ was used to denote the 'throat' as being the
organ through which one 'breathed'. Cf. the corresponding roots נָשַׁף, נָשַׁב,
and נָשַׁם, as referred to below, p. 7, n. 4: and see further Dhorme, loc. cit.,
G. R. Driver, in *Z.A.W.* lii (1934), pp. 53 f.; Th. C. Vriezen, *Hoofdlijnen
der Theologie van het Oude Testament*, 2nd edit. rev. (1954), p. 214, n. 3,
E.T. by S. Neuijen, *An Outline of Old Testament Theology* (1958), p. 202,
n. 3; Eichrodt, op. cit., p. 87, n. 77.

[2] See, however, 2 Sam. i. 9 and Job xli. 12 f. (EVV. 20 f.). For the former,
cf. the only other example of the unusual grammatical construction which it
presents (i.e. עוֹד with full substantival force?), namely Job xxvii. 3, where
the corresponding noun is the ordinary one for 'breath' (נְשָׁמָה). Thus it seems
possible that we are here dealing with an idiom, and that in the passage under
discussion Saul is represented as asking that he may be given the *coup de
grâce* (cf. T. H. Robinson, in *E.T.* lii (1940–1), p. 117) because he is still able
to draw breath. The second passage is that which occurs in the famous
description of the crocodile, i.e.:

    Out of his nostrils there cometh smoke,
        Like a pot that is heated and ⌜aboil⌝.
    His נֶפֶשׁ setteth coals ablaze,
        And a flame cometh out of his mouth.

Here the EVV. render נֶפֶשׁ by 'breath' (cf. V *halitus eius*); and this is the
accepted rendering. Cf., for example, S. R. Driver and G. B. Gray, I.C.C.
(1921), C. J. Ball, *The Book of Job* (1922), P. (E.) Dhorme, E.B. (1926),
G. Hölscher, H.A.T., 2nd edit. rev. (1952), A. Weiser, A.T.D., 3rd edit.
(1959), C. Larcher, S.B.J., 2nd edit. rev. (1957), H. Junker, Echt.B. (1959);
also H. W. Robinson, in *The People and the Book*, p. 356, and E. Schmitt,
Leben in den Weisheitsbüchern Job, Sprüche und Jesus Sirach (1954), p. 28, n. 6.
Nevertheless the reference to 'mouth' in the parallel stichos (as in Isa. v. 14,
above) suggests that נֶפֶשׁ may well have the meaning 'throat': cf. now
N. H. Tur-Sinai (H. Torczyner), *The Book of Job: a New Commentary*

of a parallel in the case of the term אַף, which could be
used equally well of the 'nostril' and of that quick nasal
breathing which is indicative of 'anger'.[1] Further, the view
that נֶפֶשׁ, besides meaning 'throat' or 'neck', may have been
used of 'breath' seems to be reinforced by the fact that in
Arabic the cognate term نَفْس has precisely this meaning.[2]
Moreover, as we shall have occasion to note again presently,
loss of vitality in any degree, from simple despondency to
death itself, is idiomatically expressed as the breathing out
of the נֶפֶשׁ,[3] just as the recovery of one's vitality during a
period of rest, or a 'breathing-space' as it may be called, is
indicated by the verb *Niph'al* from the same root.[4] These
earlier meanings of the term נֶפֶשׁ, however, have become
obscured through its use (somewhat like the Latin *animal*
-*alis*, √*anima*) to denote the more obviously animate forms
of life, i.e. animal life in general[5] or, more specifically and

---

(1957), *in loc.* Finally one should note the view that נֶפֶשׁ is used with the
meaning 'odour' or 'perfume' (as being a form of 'breath') in the much
disputed passages, Prov. xxvii. 9 and Isa. iii. 20: cf. (in addition to the com-
mentaries) G. R. Driver, in *Z.A.W.* lii (1934), pp. 53 f., and *Z.A.W.* lv
(1937), pp. 69 f.

[1] Cf., for example, Dürr, op. cit., p. 269; and see below, p. 49, n. 4.

[2] Cf. نَفْس = 'soul', 'self', 'person'.

[3] Jer. xv. 9; Job xi. 20, xxxi. 39: see further Driver–Gray and Dhorme,
op. cit., *in loc.*

[4] Exod. xxiii. 12 (E), xxxi. 17 (P); 2 Sam. xvi. 14. Cf. נָשַׁף, 'to blow':
also, with variation of the labial, נָשַׁב, 'to blow', and נָשַׁם, 'to pant, breathe',
whence נְשָׁמָה, the ordinary word for 'breath' (as below, p. 27, n. 6). See
Becker, op. cit., pp. 99 ff. Note, too, that אֶשְׁנָב, 'window', is probably to be
connected with *√שָׁנַב or, better, by metathesis with √נשׁב, as denoting that
through which the wind may blow: cf., for example, J. H. Hospers, in *B.O.*
i (1943–4), p. 55 (i.e. in a review of Becker's monograph), L. Köhler, in
J.S.S. i (1956), p. 17, also K.B., s.v. All in all, therefore, if the original meaning of נֶפֶשׁ was 'throat' or 'neck' (rather than 'breath'?), it appears to have
been so as denoting that part of the body through which one breathes, i.e.
the organ of expansion. Cf. the Accadian NAPĀŠU, 'to expand', which appears
to be cognate with RAPĀŠU, 'to be wide'. (The writer is indebted to Professor
G. R. Driver for this last interesting point.)

[5] נֶפֶשׁ appears to be used in this way (explicitly or implicitly) no more
than 32 times, i.e. less than 5 per cent. of the whole.

far more frequently, that which manifests itself in man.[1] Accordingly it is employed vaguely (like the English term 'soul') in a number of ways; but even so it is possible to see how the grasping of a totality asserts itself.[2]

Thus at one extreme it may be used to denote that common vital principle in man or beast which reveals itself in the form of conscious life, as when Solomon is congratulated upon having asked Yahweh for wisdom rather than the life (נֶפֶשׁ) of his enemies,[3] or when the infatuated youth is said to be lured on,[4]

> As a bird will hasten to the snare,
> Not knowing that its life (נֶפֶשׁ) is at stake.

Accordingly to smite a man in respect of the נֶפֶשׁ is to take away his life;[5] and in the last resort, as Zedekiah admits to Jeremiah, to do this is to rob a man of something which he shares with his fellows as a gift from Yahweh, for it is Yahweh 'who hath made this life of ours (אֲשֶׁר עָשָׂה־לָנוּ אֶת־הַנֶּפֶשׁ הַזֹּאת)'.[6] Indeed it is this thought of a common

---

[1] Besides being employed normally in this way with reference to man, נֶפֶשׁ is used analogously of Yahweh on 21 occasions (notably 9 times in the emotional pages of the book of Jeremiah), i.e. less than 3 per cent. of the whole. It also occurs once (and even so in no more than a simple idiomatic construction) with reference to foreign gods, i.e. Isa. xlvi. 2.

[2] H. W. Robinson distinguishes three meanings, i.e. (i) with reference to the principle of life 'without any emphasis upon what *we* should call its psychical side', (ii) 'the only one that can be called psychical in the proper sense', and (iii) that in which the term 'denotes "self", or the personal pronoun'; and he finds it possible to assign all 754 occurrences of the term to one or another of these three classes, in fact 282, 249, and 223 respectively. See *The Christian Doctrine of Man*, pp. 16 f., *The People and the Book*, pp. 355 ff. The present writer would agree that each of these meanings may be distinguished in certain passages, but finds the meaning of the term as a whole far too fluid to be able to accept so definite a classification. The reader should find it instructive (and even entertaining) to compare the similar attempts at an exact classification made by C. A. Briggs, 'The Use of נֶפֶשׁ in the Old Testament', *J.B.L.* xvi (1897), pp. 17–30 (cf. B.D.B., s.v.), and, say, Becker, op. cit.

[3] 1 Kings iii. 11: cf. 2 Chron. i. 11.

[4] Prov. vii. 23.

[5] Gen. xxxvii. 21 (J); Deut. xix. 6, 11; Jer. xl. 14, 15.

[6] *lit.* 'who hath made for us this life', Jer. xxxviii. 16: cf. Gen. ix. 4–6 (P), as cited below, p. 9, n. 2.

life vouchsafed by Yahweh and identifiable with the blood
(for the blood is said to be or to contain the נֶפֶשׁ)[1] which
requires that all blood shall be sacred to Yahweh and taboo
for man, and so is made the basis for the grim ritual of
sacrifice.[2] From this standpoint, therefore, the נֶפֶשׁ may be
distinguished from its bodily vehicle, the בָּשָׂר or 'flesh'.[3]
Accordingly at death it is described as being breathed or
poured out;[4] so that normally man is then like water which
has been spilt on the ground and cannot be gathered up
again.[5] In other words, when a person dies, the נֶפֶשׁ is said
to 'depart' (יָצָא);[6] and if in special circumstances life should
be restored to the corpse, it is then said to 'return' (שׁוּב).[7]
Nevertheless, as we proceed, we shall note the recognition
of a strong ebb and flow between these two poles, corresponding to the degree of vitality manifested by the נֶפֶשׁ
at any given time; and, as the reader will have occasion to
note more fully at a later stage in our study, this corresponds to the fact that the Israelite did not always think
in terms of a clear-cut distinction between 'life' and 'death'.[8]

Even at this extreme, however, the grasping of a totality

---

[1] Gen. ix. 4 (P); Lev. xvii. 11, 14 (H); Deut. xii. 23: cf. Pss. lxxii. 14,
xciv. 21; Prov. i. 18; Jer. ii. 34; Ezek. xxii. 27; Jonah i. 14; also Job xxiv. 12
(vide Dhorme, op. cit., *in loc.*).

[2] Gen. ix. 4–6 (P); Lev. xvii. 10–14 (H); Deut. xii. 23–25. See also p. 69.

[3] Cf. Deut. xii. 23; Isa. x. 18.

[4] For the former, see above, p. 7, n. 3: for the latter, see Ps. cxli. 8; Isa.
liii. 12. (Cf., too, Lam. ii. 12, as quoted below, p. 10.)

[5] Cf. 2 Sam. xiv. 14.

[6] Gen. xxxv. 18 (J): cf. Jer. xv. 9.

[7] 1 Kings xvii. 21 f.

[8] It is conceivable that idiomatic language of the type under discussion in
these pages might come to be used so colloquially as to lose something of its
original force. To this extent, therefore, there may well be some truth in the
argument of D. W. Thomas, 'A Consideration of some Unusual Ways of
Expressing the Superlative in Hebrew', *V.T.* iii (1953), pp. 219 ff. Nevertheless the data assembled in this monograph, taken as a whole, compel me to
add that we must beware of inferring that in, say, Judges xvi. 16 (as below,
p. 12, n. 7) we should think of Samson as being *no more than* what we should
understand if we were to say of him that he was 'tired to death' of the way
in which Delilah was behaving. At the same time I must admit the attractive-
ness of this as a rendering into current English idiom. See further, pp. 87 ff.
(esp. 95 ff.).

reveals itself in the fact that the term נֶפֶשׁ may be used with
more obvious reference to what is a comprehensive and
unified manifestation of sentient life, as when it is said of the
right kind of master that he understands the נֶפֶשׁ (i.e. the
feelings) of his beast,[1] or when the Israelites are reminded
that in view of their own experience in Egypt they are in
a position to know the נֶפֶשׁ (i.e. the feelings) of a resident
alien.[2] On the other hand, the feelings may be analysed, and
so make it possible to indicate a particular state of the נֶפֶשׁ
under any given conditions. Thus the sensations of hunger
and thirst may be attributed (explicitly or implicitly) to the
נֶפֶשׁ;[3] and this may be done in such a manner as to emphasize a shrinking or weakening of its power, as when it
is said, not merely to be shrivelled up[4] or empty,[5] but even
to faint and so to pour itself out or drain away. For example,
it is lamented of the children during the days of famine
which followed the destruction of Jerusalem in 587 B.C.
that:[6]

> They say to their mothers,
> 'Where is the corn and the wine?',
> While they swoon, like one who is wounded,
> In the city's broad places,
> While their נֶפֶשׁ doth drain away
> Against their mothers' bosom.

---

[1] Prov. xii. 10.   [2] Exod. xxiii. 9 (JE).

[3] Cf. Num. xi. 6 (J); Ps. cvii. 5, 9; Prov. vi. 30, x. 3, xix. 15, xxv. 25; Isa.
xxix. 8, xxxii. 6, lviii. 10 (note the parallelism): also (figuratively) Pss. xlii. 3
(EVV. 2), lxiii. 2 (EVV. 1); Jer. xxxi. 25. Cf., too, the passages cited below,
p. 13, n. 2 , p. 14, n. 1, on the expressed *desire* of the נֶפֶשׁ for food and drink;
also Deut. xxiv. 6, i.e. for the recognition that the נֶפֶשׁ is dependent upon
food for its preservation.

[4] Num. xi. 6 (J). See also, perhaps, with regard to this shrinking of the
נֶפֶשׁ, Ps. cvii. 9 and Isa. xxix. 8; for there is reason to believe that the idea
underlying the form שׁוֹקֵקָה, which occurs in both these passages, may be
that of 'contraction'. Cf. (although the present writer is unable to accept the
further view that נֶפֶשׁ in both these cases has the meaning 'throat') Dhorme,
L'Emploi métaphorique,&c., pp. 19, n. 2, and 154; and Dürr, op. cit., p. 265,
n. 1.

[5] Isa. xxix. 8, xxxii. 6. Cf. Prov. vi. 30; Eccles. vi. 7: also (fig.) Jer. xxxi. 25.

[6] Lam. ii. 12. Cf. Ps. cvii. 5: also Prov. xxv. 25; Isa. xxix. 8; and (fig.)
Ps. cxliii. 6; Jer. xxxi. 25.

Contrariwise, when such lack of nourishment is met, the vitality of the נֶפֶשׁ is restored; in other words, it becomes possible for the נֶפֶשׁ to return (שׁוּב√) to fuller life. And here again it is the scene of famine in Jerusalem, following its destruction by the Babylonians, which has furnished us with an illustration; for the poet, in lamenting the city's fate, says:[1]

> All her people are groaning,
> Are seeking bread;
> They barter their treasures for food
> To bring back the נֶפֶשׁ.

Similarly various emotional states are attributed to the נֶפֶשׁ, as when it is said to be distressed[2] or troubled,[3] and thus the prey of bitter feelings.[4] Under such conditions (much the same as under those which give rise to the sensations of hunger and thirst) the נֶפֶשׁ may be said to waste or pine away,[5] to melt or to faint,[6] and indeed to drain away;[7] and we have already seen that loss of vitality in any degree, from simple despondency to death itself, may be expressed idiomatically in terms of the breathing out of the נֶפֶשׁ.[8] In such circumstances the נֶפֶשׁ needs to be comforted, in

---

[1] Lam. i. 11: cf. verse 19 and (fig.) Ps. xxiii. 3.

[2] Gen. xlii. 21 (E); Ps. xxxi. 8.

[3] Pss. vi. 4 (EVV. 3), xlii. 6, 12 (EVV. 5, 11), xliii. 5; Isa. xv. 4, liii. 11.

[4] Judges xviii. 25; 1 Sam. i. 10, xxii. 2, xxx. 6; 2 Sam. xvii. 8; 2 Kings iv. 27; Job iii. 20, vii. 11, x. 1, xxi. 25, xxvii. 2; Prov. xxxi. 6; Isa. xxxviii. 15; Ezek. xxvii. 31: cf., too, Prov. xiv. 10.

[5] Lev. xxvi. 16 (H); Deut. xxviii. 65; 1 Sam. ii. 33; Pss. lxxxiv. 3 (EVV. 2), cxix. 81: cf. Ps. xxxi. 10 (EVV. 9).

[6] Pss. cvii. 26 (but see P. Joüon, in *Biblica* vii (1926), pp. 165 ff.), cxix. 28 (but see G. R. Driver, in *J.T.S.* xxxiv (1933), pp. 384 f.); Jer. iv. 31; Jonah ii. 8 (EVV. 7).

[7] Job xxx. 16. As in Lam. ii. 12 (quoted above), this use of the *Hithpaʿēl* of שָׁפַךְ serves to emphasize the disintegration or collapse of the נֶפֶשׁ; and one may compare the use of the same form once again in Lam. iv. 1, where it is employed figuratively to describe the scenes of destruction in Jerusalem in terms of the city's *scattered* wealth. This is rather different from the use of the *Qal* (with נֶפֶשׁ as its object) to denote the release of one's pent-up feelings, i.e. 1 Sam. i. 15; Ps. xlii. 5 (EVV. 4). Cf. the pouring out of (i) the heart (Ps. lxii. 9 (EVV. 8); Lam. ii. 19), and (ii) one's complaint (Pss. cii. 1 (EVV. title), cxlii. 3 (EVV. 2)).

[8] See above, p. 7, n. 3.

order that under these conditions also (as under the more obviously physical conditions of starvation and famine) it may be able to return (שׁוּב√) to fuller life; for man does not 'live' by bread alone.[1] Once more it is the scene of destruction in Jerusalem, following the capture of the city by the Babylonians, which provides us with a clear illustration; for an eyewitness of the scene, speaking emotionally in the name of the city, says:[2]

> This is why I keep weeping,
> Why mine eyes run with tears;
> For I have no comforter at hand,
> No one to bring back my נֶפֶשׁ.

Corresponding to this there is a recognized oscillation in mood, so that the נֶפֶשׁ may be said to grieve (or weep)[3] but also to be glad (or rejoice),[4] to have a sinking feeling of despair[5] but also to hope,[6] to be impatient[7] but also to be patient,[8] and above all (according as one finds that an attitude of repulsion or attraction is aroused) to hate[9] but also to love,[10] and, more often and far more emphatically, to loathe[11] but also to desire.

The last point, i.e. the recognition that the נֶפֶשׁ is subject

---

[1] The reader will recognize the borrowed phrase, i.e. Deut. viii. 3; Matt. iv. 4; Luke iv. 4.

[2] Lam. i. 16. Cf. Ruth iv. 15; Ps. xix. 8 (EVV. 7); Prov. xxv. 13: also Job xxxiii. 30 (see below, pp. 90 ff.). For Ps. xxiii. 3, see above, p. 11, n. 1.

[3] Job xix. 2, xxx. 25; Isa. xix. 10; Jer. xiii. 17: cf. Job xiv. 22; also (vide S) Ps. xiii. 3 (EVV. 2).

[4] Pss. xxxv. 9, lxxi. 23, lxxxvi. 4; Isa. lxi. 10: cf. Pss. xxxiv. 3 (EVV. 2), xciv. 19, cxxxviii. 3 (?), cxlvi. 1; Prov. xxix. 17; Isa. lv. 2, lxvi. 3: also (of God) Isa. xlii. 1. Cf., too, Ezek. xxv. 6, 15, xxxvi. 5.

[5] Pss. xlii. 6, 7, 12 (EVV. 5, 6, 11), xliii. 5; Lam. iii. 20: cf. Pss. xliv. 26 (EVV. 25), cxix. 28.

[6] Pss. xlii. 6, 12 (EVV. 5, 11), xliii. 5.

[7] Num. xxi. 4 (JE); Judges xvi. 16: also (of God) Judges x. 16; Zech. xi. 8.

[8] Job vi. 11: cf., for example, Driver–Gray, op. cit., as against Dhorme, op. cit., *in loc.*

[9] 2 Sam. v. 8 (Q): also (of God) Ps. xi. 5; Isa. i. 14.

[10] Song of Sol. i. 7, iii. 1, 2, 3, 4: also (of God) Jer. xii. 7.

[11] Lev. xxvi. 15, 43 (both H); Num. xxi. 5 (JE); Job x. 1, xxxiii. 20; Ps. cvii. 18; Zech. xi. 8: also (of God) Lev. xxvi. 11, 30 (both H); Prov. vi. 16; Jer. xiv. 19. Cf. (for the resultant alienation of the נֶפֶשׁ) Ezek. xxiii. 17, 22, 28: also (of God) Jer. vi. 8; Ezek. xxiii. 18 (*bis*).

to various forms of attraction which move it to activity in one direction or another through the excitation of desire, introduces one of the outstanding features in the use of the term. Its employment in this way comes out clearly, for example, in its frequent association with אוה√;[1] for it is used in this connexion to express a wide range of such activity from the simple desire for food[2] (or, say, the eagerness of a king to extend his sovereignty)[3] to the worshipper's longing for fellowship with Yahweh.[4] The same idea is occasionally expressed, not by saying explicitly that the נֶפֶשׁ has any such desire (אוה√), but by speaking, rather, of directing (*lit.* lifting up)[5] the נֶפֶשׁ towards a particular end, as when one's employee is thus said to show a legitimate desire for his wages,[6] or the exile is similarly said to yearn for his homeland,[7] or the believer gives expression in this way to his longing for a response from Yahweh.[8] In these circumstances, therefore, it is no matter for surprise that the term נֶפֶשׁ is often used by itself with an obvious emphasis upon desire in some form or another. This is especially true, once again, of the desire for food; and we may compare the use of the corresponding Arabic term نَفْس to indicate what we should call one's appetite.[9] Indeed in

---

[1] The *Pi'ēl* (אִוָּה) and the noun אַוָּה, for example, are used almost exclusively with נֶפֶשׁ.

[2] Deut. xii. 15, 20 (*bis*), 21, xiv. 26; 1 Sam. ii. 16; Job xxxiii. 20; Mic. vii. 1: cf. Deut. xviii. 6: also (of mating-time in the animal world) Jer. ii. 24. Cf., too, Prov. xiii. 4, 19.

[3] 2 Sam. iii. 21; 1 Kings xi. 37. For other (more general) examples, see 1 Sam. xxiii. 20; Ps. x. 3; Prov. xxi. 10: also (of God) Job xxiii. 13. Cf., too, Eccles. vi. 2.

[4] Isa. xxvi. 8, 9.

[5] נָשָׂא. Cf., in addition to the examples cited below, Ps. xxiv. 4; Hos. iv. 8; also Ezek. xxiv. 25. The writer is here following the usual interpretation of this expression; but it is conceivable that this idiom really goes back to the idea of 'craning one's *neck*' in a certain direction. Even so, of course, the main line of argument in this section would remain unaffected.

[6] Deut. xxiv. 15.

[7] Jer. xxii. 27, xliv. 14.

[8] Ps. cxliii. 8: cf. xxv. 1, lxxxvi. 4.

[9] e.g. in the colloquial *mâlîsh nafs*, 'I have no appetite'. Cf., too, Albright, loc. cit., apropos the corresponding use of the Ugaritic *npš*.

certain circumstances this use of the term suggests sheer greed, so that a glutton may be described in typically Semitic fashion as a בַּעַל נֶפֶשׁ, i.e. what we should call a 'past master' in this realm;[1] and it is but the same idea in a transferred sense which comes to the fore when the psalmist prays with regard to his enemies:[2]

> Let them not say in their heart, 'Aha, our desire (הֶאָח נַפְשֵׁנוּ)!'
> Let them not say, 'We have swallowed him up!'

i.e.

> Let them not say to themselves, 'Hurrah, we have what we wanted!'
> Let them not say, 'We have swallowed him up!'

Here, then, we have what is undoubtedly the most common use of the term so far as this particular connotation is concerned; but occasionally it is employed in this way with a somewhat wider force, as when it is said of treacherous men (with typical emphasis upon unity of purpose) that 'their נֶפֶשׁ is violence', i.e. (as we might say) that they are 'all out' for violence.[3] Occasionally, too, this simple use of the term shades off until the word acquires what is almost a volitional, rather than an emotional, aspect; for example, when it is laid down in the D code that, if a man should lose interest in a captive woman whom he has made his wife, he may not sell her as a slave but must let her go as she will (לְנַפְשָׁהּ).[4] In any case one can hardly fail to note that, where this particular connotation appears, a certain unity of purpose (indicative of the grasping of a totality) is associated with the נֶפֶשׁ; and, as already indicated, this may show

---

[1] Prov. xxiii. 2. See further Deut. xxiii. 25 (EVV. 24); Prov. xvi. 26; Isa. lvi. 11; Hos. ix. 4. Cf., too, Deut. xiv. 26; Job vi. 7; Pss. lxiii. 6 (EVV. 5), lxxviii. 18; Prov. vi. 30, xiii. 25, xxvii. 7; Eccles. vi. 7; Isa. lv. 2, lviii. 10, 11; Jer. xxxi. 14, l. 19; Ezek. vii. 19.

[2] Ps. xxxv. 25: cf. Pss. xvii. 9, xxvii. 12, xli. 3 (EVV. 2); Ezek. xvi. 27; also Exod. xv. 9 (J).

[3] Prov. xiii. 2. For similar references of a more general kind, see Prov. xiii. 4 (*bis*), 19, xxviii. 25; Eccles. vi. 2, 3, 9; Ezek. xxiv. 21 (?), 25 (cf. p. 13, n. 5); Mic. vii. 3.

[4] Deut. xxi. 14: cf. Jer. xxxiv. 16. See also, in addition to the examples cited in the following note, Mic. vi. 7: cf. J. M. P. Smith, I.C.C. (1911), *in loc.*

itself even when the term is used with reference to a social unit of some kind rather than what we should call a mere individual. Thus Jehu, having been instigated to revolt by Elisha's messenger and wishing to warn his associates against any betrayal of his plans, says:[1]

If your נֶפֶשׁ be (*or* If it be in accordance with your נֶפֶשׁ), let no fugitive leave the city so that he may go and make the news known in Jezreel.

Here the emphasis lies upon the unity of aim, and in English the corresponding idiom would be, 'If you are of one mind, . . .' or 'If you are agreeable, . . .'. To the Israelite, however, such unity of purpose thus manifest in a group of people is simply evidence of a corporate personality rather than that of a mere individual, and so may be indicated with equal justification by the simple term נֶפֶשׁ.[2]

Further, the fact that the word נֶפֶשׁ could be used in so many different ways to denote various forms of self-expression (amounting sometimes to actual selfishness) makes it possible to understand the frequent use of this term along with a suffix to refer to one's 'person' or 'self' and thus to form the equivalent of a personal or reflexive pronoun.[3]

---

[1] 2 Kings ix. 15, i.e. אִם־יֵשׁ נַפְשְׁכֶם. The alternative rendering is that suggested by certain manuscripts, i.e. אִם־יֵשׁ אֶת־נַפְשְׁכֶם: cf. Gen. xxiii. 8 (P).

[2] For the expression 'corporate personality', see *The One and the Many in the Israelite Conception of God*, p. 12, n. 2, 2nd edit., p. 8, n. 2; and note incidentally that the criticism passed by L. H. Brockington, in *J.T.S.* xlvii (1946), p. 3, n. 6, on the present writer's argument in the context of the foregoing reference is based upon a failure to realize that the term under discussion may be used collectively in the singular with just as much indication of the grasping of a totality as when it is used of an individual.

[3] The instances of this use are undoubtedly many. For example, Briggs, op. cit., pp. 21 ff. (cf. B.D.B., s.v.), claims that there are 70 cases of the former and 53 of the latter, i.e. 123 in all, while Becker, op. cit., p. 117, discovers a total of 135. Robinson again (as cited above, p. 8, n. 2) claims that altogether there are 223 instances; but he is obviously including examples of the somewhat different use discussed in the next paragraph. The present writer has already commented upon the difficulty of making a precise analysis (loc. cit.); and the following typical examples of apparent ambiguity will serve to illustrate the point as it affects both forms. (i) Song of Sol. v. 6: נַפְשִׁי יָצְאָה בְדַבְּרוֹ. A.V. 'my soul failed when he spake', R.V. 'My soul had failed me

This may be seen quite clearly on consulting the many cases of poetic parallelism in which such a form as we are now discussing is balanced by another form with a corresponding pronominal element, i.e. a suffix or such as is involved in the inflexion of the verb. Thus (to take a simple example), when Job says,[1]

> Have I not wept for him who was having a hard time?
> Did not my נֶפֶשׁ grieve for the poor?

—the second stichos comes very close to meaning,

> Did not I personally grieve for the poor?
> or Did not I myself grieve for the poor?

[mgn.: Heb. *went forth*] when he spake', and so again R.S.V. 'My soul failed me when he spoke'. This is taken to mean (in line with the renderings of EVV.) that the speaker had fainted when she heard her lover's voice. Cf., for example, A. Harper, C.B. (1902), *in loc*. On the other hand, however, we may not dismiss too readily the view sponsored by F. Hitzig, K.e.H. (1855), *in loc*. (and accepted now by K.B., s.v.; H. Ringgren, A.T.D. (1958); W. Rudolph, K.A.T. (1962); and, as a possible alternative, by T. J. Meek, I.B. (1956)), that the consonantal text of the last word should be associated with the Arabic دَبَرَ, e.g. IV, 'to turn back'; for this seems to fit the context much better than the foregoing traditional interpretation, if we then take the sentence as a whole to mean 'I myself went out on his turning back'. In fact it is difficult to resist the conclusion that the normal translation of this passage (as given above and, indeed, as retained by Meek, Ringgren, and Rudolph for the first part of the sentence) reveals as complete a misunderstanding of Hebrew idiom and, therefore, of this lover's natural reaction to the situation with which she was confronted in her dream as would be the case if one were to take the Hebrew of Genesis xxiv. 64 (J) to imply that, as soon as Rebekah caught sight of Isaac, she fell off her camel (וַתִּפֹּל מֵעַל הַגָּמָל)! (ii) Judges ix. 17: וַיַּשְׁלֵךְ אֶת־נַפְשׁוֹ מִנֶּגֶד. A.V. 'and adventured his life far [mgn.: Heb. *cast his life*]', R.V. 'and adventured his life [mgn.: Heb. *cast his life before him*]'. This is taken to mean (as in EVV.) that Gideon hazarded or risked his life, i.e. and thus saved the people of Shechem from the Midianites (vide comm., *in loc.*: and cf. now R.S.V.); but a more likely meaning appears to be that he achieved this result because, as we should say, 'he flung himself to the fore'.

[1] xxx. 25. Cf., *inter alia*, Pss. xxx. 4 (EVV. 3), xxxiii. 19, xxxv. 7, xli. 5 (EVV. 4), lvii. 2 (EVV. 1), lix. 4 (EVV. 3), lxix. 19 (EVV. 18), lxxxviii. 15 (EVV. 14), xciv. 17, cxix. 167, cxxi. 7, cxxiv. 7, cxxx. 5, cxliii. 11, 12; Prov. xviii. 7, xxiii. 14; Isa. xlii. 1, xliii. 4, lxi. 10, lxvi. 3. Cf., too, Ps. iii. 3; Eccles. vii. 28; Isa. iii. 9: and (of God) Jer. v. 9, 29, ix. 8, xiv. 19. See also 1 Kings xx. 32 and Jer. xxxviii. 17, as cited below, p. 18, nn. 5 and 6. Note incidentally that the rare construction in Isa. xxvi. 9 and Jer. iv. 19 is rather different from that which is here under discussion: cf. G.K., § 144*m*.

Similarly a form of this kind is sometimes used as the object of a verb, not merely to provide the equivalent of a reflexive form, but actually in conjunction with such a form (i.e. as its obvious parallel);[1] and this is wholly in line with the fact that one may employ the same idiom in order to speak of self-deception[2] and self-denial,[3] of congratulating oneself[4] and of laying oneself under an obligation,[5] and so on.[6] Hence (to quote but one example of this reflexive meaning), it could be said quite simply of David and Jonathan that the personality (נֶפֶשׁ) of the latter was so bound up with that of the former that he loved him 'as himself (כְּנַפְשׁוֹ)'.[7] Accordingly, in all the foregoing cases (as in the many other examples which are available)[8] the emphasis again lies upon the complete personality, just as when Job rebukes his tormentors by saying,[9]

> I also could speak like you,
> If only your נֶפֶשׁ were in the place of my נֶפֶשׁ;

for in English this is to be rendered simply (but in a way wholly appropriate to the Hebrew),

> I also could speak like you,
> If only you were in my place
> (*or* If only you were I).

Nevertheless, as one might expect in view of what has been said about the ascription of emotional states to the נֶפֶשׁ, it

---

[1] Lev. xi. 43–44 (P); Deut. iv. 9.   [2] Jer. xxxvii. 9.

[3] Cf. Lev. xvi. 29, 31 (P), xxiii. 27, 32 (H); Num. xxix. 7 (P), xxx. 14 (EVV. 13: P); Ps. xxxv. 13; Isa. lviii. 3, 5.

[4] Ps. xlix. 19 (EVV. 18): cf. Deut. xxix. 18 (EVV. 19).

[5] Num. xxx. 3, 5 (*bis*), 6, 7, 8, 9, 10, 11, 12, 13 (all P).

[6] Cf. (i) the use of נַפְשִׁי in the self-exhortation of the poet, i.e. Gen. xlix. 6; Judges v. 21; Pss. xlii. 6, 12 (EVV. 5, 11), xliii. 5, ciii. 1, 2, 22, civ. 1, 35, cxvi. 7, cxlvi. 1: and (ii) the use of בְּנַפְשׁוֹ to denote the way in which Yahweh swears 'by Himself', i.e. Jer. li. 14; Amos vi. 8.

[7] 1 Sam. xviii. 1 (cf. verse 3). See further (for such intimate association of one נֶפֶשׁ with another) Gen. xliv. 30 (J); 1 Sam. xx. 17, xxv. 29: also Deut. xiii. 7 (EVV. 6).

[8] These are so numerous that the reader must be referred for further illustration to the detailed analysis offered by Briggs, loc. cit.

[9] xvi. 4.

should be borne in mind that the use of this term as a substitute for the personal pronoun often betrays a certain intensity of feeling; so that one is sometimes right to describe it (not merely as a periphrasis but) as a *pathetic* periphrasis for such a pronoun.[1] Thus, when it is used of the subject of the action in bestowing a blessing, it appears to spring from and certainly serves to accentuate the view that the speaker needs to put all his being (or, as we might say, all his 'soul') into what he says, if he is to make his words effective.[2] Again, it is the same idiomatic use of נֶפֶשׁ which springs to the lips in those times of crisis when one is brought face to face with the issues of life and death in their most urgent form. Samson, for example, employs it when he resolves to destroy his enemies and, realizing that their destruction must involve his own death, deliberately resigns himself to his fate with the words תָּמֹת נַפְשִׁי עִם־פְּלִשְׁתִּים.[3] The rendering of the English Versions (i.e. 'Let me[4] die with the Philistines') is far from doing justice to the emotional content of the original, and one is forced to admit that the Hebrew really defies anything like a satisfactory translation. Similarly when Benhadad (through his intermediaries) pleads with Ahab for his life and says תְּחִי־נָא נַפְשִׁי, there is an element of pathos in his words which is again quite lost in the rendering of the English Versions, i.e. 'I pray thee, let me live'. Nevertheless, that the original essentially means no more than this is indicated by Ahab's simple words of surprise הַעוֹדֶנּוּ חַי, i.e. 'Is he still alive?'[5]

Finally, so close a connexion with the verb חָיָה and, indeed, so widespread a connexion[6] serves to remind one of

---

[1] Cf., for example, S. R. Driver, I.C.C., 3rd edit. (1902), on Deut. xii. 20; also *The Parallel Psalter* (1898), pp. 459 f.

[2] Cf. Gen. xxvii. 4, 19, 25, 31 (J); and see below, pp. 58 ff.

[3] Judges xvi. 30: cf. Num. xxiii. 10 (E).

[4] A.V. mgn.: 'Heb. *my soul*'.   [5] 1 Kings xx. 32.

[6] See further (for the *Qal*) Gen. xii. 13, xix. 20 (both J); Ps. cxix. 175; Isa. lv. 3; Jer. xxxviii. 17, 20: (for the *Pi'ēl*) 1 Kings xx. 31; Ps. xxii. 30 (EVV. 29); Ezek. xiii. 19, xviii. 27: (for the *Hiph'îl*) Gen. xix. 19 (J). Cf., too, the familiar form of the oath חֵי נַפְשְׁךָ (e.g. 1 Sam. i. 26, and so often); and see below, pp. 95 ff.

the fact that this use of the term נֶפֶשׁ to denote one's 'person' or 'self' as a centre of consciousness and unit of vital power has an exact counterpart in the J narrative of the Creation, which tells how Yahweh first modelled a man out of earth or clay and then breathed into the nostrils of this figure, so that *it* became a נֶפֶשׁ חַיָּה, i.e. as we should say, 'a living person' (EVV. 'a living soul').[1] As it happens, the foregoing passage is the only one which offers an example of this particular expression; and the reason is clear. The introduction of the adjective חַיָּה ('living') in so emphatic a way was obviously rendered necessary by the context.[2] Accordingly the use of the term נֶפֶשׁ in this passage is not markedly different from that in which it is often employed by itself to denote any human being, man or woman, as a 'person'.

---

[1] Gen. ii. 7. Cf. *The One and the Many in the Israelite Conception of God*, pp. 5 f., 2nd edit., pp. 1 f.; and note that R.S.V. has adopted the rendering 'a living being'.

[2] Thus the expression as a whole must not be confused with the similar expression נֶפֶשׁ חַיָּה, which is used with a collective force to denote creatures of the 'animal' world in the narrow sense, i.e. other than man. With the exception of Gen. ii. 19 (J), the latter expression is peculiar to P and the book of Ezekiel, i.e. Gen. i. 20, 21, 24, ix. 10, 12, 15, 16 (all P); Lev. xi. 10, 46 (both P); Ezek. xlvii. 9; and it has long been recognized that its appearance in Gen. ii. 19, where it is syntactically difficult, is due to a gloss. Cf., for example, H. Gunkel, H.K., 3rd edit. rev. (1910) and J. Skinner, I.C.C. (1910), *in loc.* In this case, as is clear from the definite form of the expression (i.e. נֶפֶשׁ הַחַיָּה: Gen. i. 21, ix. 10; Lev. xi. 10, 46), the second component is not the adjective חַי ('living') in its feminine form but the noun חַיָּה (*lit.* 'living thing', i.e. 'animal' in the above-mentioned narrow sense) with its collective connotation. The expression as a whole corresponds to that in which the noun אָדָם ('man' or 'mankind') is similarly appended to נֶפֶשׁ in the form נֶפֶשׁ אָדָם to refer specifically and collectively to human beings. See Num. xxxi. 35, 40, 46 (all P); 1 Chron. v. 21; Ezek. xxvii. 13. Cf., too, Lev. xxiv. 17 (in antithesis to verse 18: both H): and note again the fact that the corresponding expression is peculiar to P and the book of Ezekiel. As may be seen from the passages cited, however, this distinction is rare, being used only to effect a contrast or for the sake of emphasis; and, as will be seen from what follows, the same circles which draw this distinction normally find it sufficient to use the term נֶפֶשׁ by itself in this sense. On the other hand, there does not appear to be any example of the use of נֶפֶשׁ *by itself* with exclusive reference to the animal world (i.e. in the narrow sense).

A simple but typical example is furnished by the poet who claims that, despite appearances,[1]

> Yahweh is good to those who wait for Him,
> To the נֶפֶשׁ that seeketh Him.

Another (and common) example is that preserved in the legal phraseology of H and P whereby provision is made as to what shall happen if any 'person' (נֶפֶשׁ) acts or fails to act in a given way; e.g. that if anyone offends against a particular law, then 'that person' (הַנֶּפֶשׁ הַהִוא)[2] shall be cut off from society.[3] Sometimes, again, the term נֶפֶשׁ is used collectively in this sense, as in the statement:[4]

> And Abram took Sarai his wife, and Lot his brother's son, and all their property which they had gained and the persons whom they had acquired (וְאֶת־הַנֶּפֶשׁ אֲשֶׁר־עָשׂוּ) in Haran, and they went forth to go into the land of Canaan.

As often as not, however, this use occurs in enumerations; e.g. when Moses reminds the Israelites of their remarkable growth as a people by saying (according to the book of Deuteronomy):[5]

---

[1] Lam. iii. 25. The examples of this use are undoubtedly frequent. For instance, Briggs, op. cit., pp. 23 f. (cf. B.D.B., s.v.), claims that in all there are 144 examples, while Becker, op. cit., p. 117, finds at least 109 (omitting, for instance, those passages in which the term has the meaning 'corpse', as discussed below). Moreover, as Briggs points out, they occur for the most part in H, P, and the work of related writers, e.g. the book of Ezekiel.

[2] *Sic.*

[3] So (in full) Lev. vii. 20, 21, 27 (all P); Num. xv. 30 f. (P). Cf., *inter alia*, (a) Lev. ii. 1, iv. 2, 27, v. 1, 2, 4, 15, 17, 21 (EVV. vi. 2) (all P), xx. 6, xxii. 6 (both H); Num. xv. 27 (P): (b) Gen. xvii. 14 (P); Exod. xii. 15, 19, xxxi. 14 (all P); Lev. xix. 8, xxii. 3 (both H); Num. ix. 13, xix. 13, 20 (all P): cf. Lev. vii. 25 (P), xvii. 10, xx. 6, xxiii. 29, 30 (all H); also the similar use of the plural in xviii. 29 (H), as below, p. 21, n. 1. Amongst the other examples which are available to illustrate the use of the singular with an individual (i.e. not a collective) force, the following are the most interesting and instructive: Lev. xxii. 11 (H); Num. v. 6, xxxi. 19, xxxv. 30 (all P); Deut. xxiv. 7, xxvii. 25; Ezek. xviii. 4, 20, xxxiii. 6.

[4] Gen. xii. 5 (P). Cf. Gen. xiv. 21; Joshua x. 28, 30, 32, 35, 37, 39, xi. 11 (cf. verse 14) (all D); Jer. xliii. 6; Ezek. xxii. 25: also Ezek. xxvii. 13 (as above, p. 19, n. 2).

[5] x. 22. The somewhat free rendering of the phrase under discussion marks an attempt to convey the force of (i) the emphatic position of the original, and (ii) the *bêth essentiae*. Cf. Gen. xlvi. 15, 18, 22, 25, 26, 27 (all P); Exod.

Thy fathers went down into Egypt a mere seventy persons (בְּשִׁבְעִים נֶפֶשׁ); and now Yahweh thy God hath made thee like the stars of heaven in multitude.

On the other hand, the collective singular sometimes gives way to the full plural form of the noun, as in the account of Esau's settlement in the mountain country of Seir, i.e.:[1]

And Esau took his wives, and his sons, and his daughters, and all the persons of his household (וְאֶת־כָּל־נַפְשׁוֹת בֵּיתוֹ), and his cattle and all his beasts, and all his possessions which he had gained in the land of Canaan, and went into ⌜the⌝ land ⌜of Seir⌝ away from his brother Jacob.

Finally, from such a use of the term נֶפֶשׁ to denote a *living* person it is no far step to its use with reference to a *dead* one, i.e. a 'corpse'; and indeed this step is actually taken. The examples are restricted to a few passages in H and P and a single passage in the book of Haggai, but they are sufficiently numerous and in some cases so clearly defined as to make the transition in meaning perfectly clear. Accordingly, while one may speak of a נֶפֶשׁ מֵת, i.e. 'the נֶפֶשׁ of one that is dead' (in short 'a dead body'),[2] such a

---

i. 5 (P); Num. xxxi. 35b, 40b (both P); Jer. lii. 29, 30: also Num. xxxi. 35a, 40a, 46 (all P); 1 Chron. v. 21 (as above, p. 19, n. 2).

[1] Gen. xxxvi. 6 (P), emended *ad fin.* in accordance with S. Cf. Exod. xii. 4, xvi. 16 (both P); Lev. xviii. 29 (H), xxvii. 2 (P); Num. xix. 18 (P); 2 Kings xii. 5 (EVV. 4); Ezek. xiii. 17–23, xviii. 4, xxii. 27. In several instances the plural form appears to be due to an emphasis upon individuality which is made necessary by the context. Further, in the case of the remarkable passage Ezek. xiii. 17–23 we need to bear in mind the indefinable 'extensions' of the personality to which the present writer has already drawn attention, i.e. in *The One and the Many in the Israelite Conception of God*, pp. 6 ff., 2nd edit., pp. 2 ff.; and *The Cultic Prophet in Ancient Israel* (1944), p. 19, n. 6, 2nd edit. rev. (1962), p. 18, n. 4. Accordingly, while G. A. Cooke, I.C.C. (1936), *in loc.*, is probably right in insisting that here, too, the term נְפָשׁוֹת denotes 'persons', we must beware of dismissing so easily as he does the views of J. G. Frazer and S. A. Cook with regard to the interpretation of this passage. Even though we may adopt the rendering 'persons' as the most suitable (or the least unsuitable!) in this connexion, we must not forget that in the ultimate we are still dealing, not with the English term 'person', but with the Hebrew term נֶפֶשׁ and all that this may connote.

[2] Num. vi. 6 (P): cf. Lev. xxi. 11 (H), esp. LXX, S; also Num. xix. 11, 13 (both P). The last passage in particular makes it quite clear that the reference must be to the נֶפֶשׁ as something with which one can come into physical

definition is usually found unnecessary, and it is sufficient
to speak quite simply of a נֶפֶשׁ when one wishes to refer to
a 'corpse'.[1] This being the case, we have travelled full circle
in our examination of the term under discussion; for it thus
reverts to a purely physical meaning such as we have already
observed in its use to denote the 'throat' or 'neck'.[2] What
is more, נֶפֶשׁ thus offers an excellent example of the semantic polarization which is so interesting a feature of the
Semitic languages;[3] for, as we have seen, at one extreme
it may denote that vital principle in man which animates the
human body and reveals itself in the form of conscious
life, and at the other extreme it may denote the corpse from
which such conscious life has departed!

contact, i.e. not the 'soul' of the dead as some sort of ghostly phenomenon.
Cf. G. B. Gray, I.C.C. (1903), *in loc.* (and on verse 11). For the present
writer's opinion of the argument advanced by M. Seligson, *The Meaning of*
נפשׁ מת *in the Old Testament*, S.O. xvi. 2 (1951), who claims that the
expression in question refers to 'the disease and death demon which is still
supposed to hover around the body but which now is called "the potency in
the dead" ' (p. 82), see *J.B.L.* lxxi (1952), pp. 257–9. Cf. G. Widengren, in
V.T. iv (1954), pp. 97–102: and, apropos the author's argument as a whole,
see also what is said above, p. 3, n. 4, about the questionable use of the term
'soul' in works of this kind.

    [1] Lev. xix. 28, xxi. 1, xxii. 4 (all H); Num. v. 2, vi. 11, ix. 6, 7, 10, xix.
11, 13 (all P); Hag. ii. 13. Occasionally the fact that the reference is to a
'human corpse' is made explicit by defining it as a נֶפֶשׁ אָדָם, i.e. Num. ix. 6,
7, xix. 11: cf., too, xix. 13.

    [2] In post-Biblical Hebrew, like the Aramaic נפשׁא and the Syriac ܢܰܦܫܳܐ,
it is even used to denote a sepulchral monument or tombstone.

    [3] This phenomenon was known to Arabic lexicographers as a ضِدّ, i.e.
a word which has two contrary meanings, such as جَوْن which may mean
either 'black' or 'white'. Cf. E. W. Lane, *An Arabic–English Lexicon* (1863–
86), s.v.; and see further, for example, T. Nöldeke, 'Wörter mit Gegensinn
(Aḍdād)', in *Neue Beiträge zur semitischen Sprachwissenschaft* (1910), pp. 67–
108, where many possible cases of such semantic polarization within several
languages of the Semitic group are discussed at some length. Perhaps the
most striking examples within the group as a whole are those afforded by
(i) the Hebrew אָבָה, 'to be willing', which corresponds to the Arabic أَبَى,
'to refuse'; and (ii) the Hebrew יָשַׁב, 'to sit', which corresponds to the Arabic
وَثَبَ, 'to leap'. (This statement ignores dialectal variations, of course: cf.
Lane, op. cit., s.v.; also G. R. Driver, in *J.T.S.* xxxiv (1933), p. 379.)

II

The importance which is thus attached to the breath in arriving at a conception of man has a close parallel in the use of the term רוּחַ.[1] Etymologically this is connected with a root which occurs in all but the eastern branch of the Semitic languages, and everywhere points to an initial awareness of air in motion, particularly 'wind'.[2] At any rate,

[1] As already indicated (p. 3, n. 4, *ad fin.*), the ensuing discussion is based upon an independent examination of all the examples of the use of this term which are to be found in the Old Testament; but, in addition to consulting the relevant articles in the standard dictionaries and encyclopaedias, the reader should compare, say, C. A. Briggs, 'The Use of רוח in the Old Testament', *J.B.L.* xix (1900), pp. 132–45 (cf. B.D.B., s.v.): W. R. Schoemaker, 'The Use of רוּחַ in the Old Testament, and of Πνεῦμα in the New Testament', *J.B.L.* xxiii (1904), pp. 13–67: H. W. Robinson, *The Christian Doctrine of Man*, pp. 17 ff.; 'Hebrew Psychology', in *The People and the Book*, pp. 358 ff.; *The Christian Experience of the Holy Spirit* (1928), pp. 12 ff.: E. D. Burton, *Spirit, Soul, and Flesh* (1918), pp. 53 ff.: Pedersen, *Israel I–II*, pp. 77 ff., E.T., pp. 102 ff.: Eichrodt, *Theologie des Alten Testaments*, ii, pp. 65 ff., ii–iii, 4th edit., pp. 85 ff.: Jean, in *R.H.R.* cxxi (1940), pp. 118 ff.: and now J. H. Scheepers, *Die gees van God en die gees van die mens in die Ou Testament* (1960): D. Lys, *'Rûach': Le Souffle dans l'Ancien Testament. Enquête anthropologique à travers l'histoire théologique d'Israël*, E.H.P.R. 56 (1962), i.e. a companion piece to the work by the same author which is cited above, p. 3, n. 4. Of course, reference might easily be made to a considerable body of literature touching this subject (cf., for example, the bibliography supplied by Scheepers, op. cit., pp. 323 ff.); but in the present writer's opinion the usual treatment of this term tends to suffer from the fact that it is normally examined under pressure of (i) a predominant interest in its application to Yahweh, and (ii) a more general occupation with the Christian doctrine of the Holy Spirit. In view of the gentle criticism levelled by Eichrodt, op. cit., p. 24, n. 2, at the standpoint which I have taken up in this connexion and which I now find it even more necessary to emphasize, perhaps I should add that I hope to return to an examination of the term רוּחַ in its application to Yahweh in the work referred to in the preface to the second edition of *The One and the Many in the Israelite Conception of God*. Indeed I have made a preliminary approach to the subject in a paper entitled ' "Holy Spirit" in the Thought of Ancient Israel', which formed my presidential address before the Society for Old Testament Study at its Winter Meeting in January 1956; but, as being no more than a tentative survey of the issues involved, this remains unpublished.

[2] Cf. the summary statement in B.D.B., s.v., *ad init.* Further, in the light of the ensuing discussion (with its emphasis upon an ebb and flow in one's vitality), it should also be borne in mind that רוּחַ may well be cognate with רָוַח, 'to be wide' (cf. רֶוַח, (i) 'extent', (ii) 'relief'). Cf. the similar association of נֶפֶשׁ with the Accadian NAPĀŠU, 'to expand', and RAPĀŠU, 'to be wide', as above, p. 7, n. 4.

so far as the Old Testament is concerned, this is indisputably the most common meaning of the term רוּחַ at the purely physical stage; and this meaning is found quite freely in early and late records alike.[1] In this sense it may denote at one extreme no more than what we should call a 'whiff'[2] (or 'breath') of air,[3] in particular a gentle, refreshing breeze of the kind which sometimes springs up in the East towards sundown, and so encourages one to walk abroad after the oppressive heat of middle day.[4] On the other hand, of course, it may be far more vigorous and much less gentle, blowing hot from the east to scorch one's vineyards,[5] driving before it the straw and chaff, the dust and leaves, which lie in its path,[6] or bending to its will (as it were) the very trees of the forest which stand in its way,[7] or even darkening the sky with a portentous cloud of locusts.[8] Indeed it may reach such a pitch of violence as to sweep down upon one's dwelling and bring the walls about one's ears[9] or lash the waves of the sea into a fury of storm and shipwreck.[10]

It stands to reason, of course, that the רוּחַ, as denoting 'wind', should thus be found variable in its intensity and

[1] According to Briggs, op. cit., pp. 133–5 (cf. B.D.B., s.v.), 117 out of the 378 occurrences of the term are to be classed under this head; and, while the present writer once again finds it difficult to be so definite in the matter of classification, this figure may safely be accepted as giving a reasonably sound indication of the actual proportion. This is now largely confirmed by Scheepers, op. cit., pp. 11–33, 304 f., although he finds the proportion slightly higher, i.e. 144 examples out of 389 occurrences of the term.

[2] Cf. רֵיחַ and its parallels in Aramaic (including Syriac) and Arabic, all with the meaning 'odour' or 'scent'.

[3] Cf. Jer. ii. 24, xiv. 6; Hos. viii. 7; also Job xli. 8 (EVV. 16). In defence of the Massoretic vocalization in the case of the last passage, see, for example, Driver–Gray and Dhorme, *in loc.*

[4] Gen. iii. 8 (J): cf. xviii. 1 (J).

[5] Ezek. xvii. 10, xix. 12: cf. Jer. iv. 11; Hos. xiii. 15; Jonah iv. 8; also Ps. ciii. 16.

[6] Job xxi. 18; Pss. i. 4, xviii. 43 (EVV. 42), xxxv. 5, lxxxiii. 14 (EVV. 13); Isa. xvii. 13, xli. 15–16, lxiv. 5 (EVV. 6); Jer. iv. 11–12, xiii. 24.

[7] Isa. vii. 2.

[8] Cf. Exod. x. 13 and 19 (JE).

[9] Job i. 19; Ezek. xiii. 11, 13.

[10] Pss. xlviii. 8 (EVV. 7), cvii. 25; Ezek. xxvii. 26; Jonah i. 4.

changeable in its ways; but the recognition of this fact enables us to understand why the term could also be used in a secondary sense, broadly corresponding to the term 'spirit' (by which it is often rendered in the English Versions), in order to denote the equally varied behaviour of human beings. Thus in the early period it seems to have been used to refer to anyone (and especially an individual like Elijah)[1] who by physical energy or mental alertness revealed that, as we say, he or she was 'full of life'.[2] In fact, as we have already noticed in discussing the term נֶפֶשׁ,[3] man's life was found to be in a state of ebb and flow; and just as the רוּחַ, *qua* 'wind', was observed to rise and sink, so this ebb and flow in one's vitality was described in terms of the absence or presence of רוּחַ. Thus it is said of Jacob, for example, when he recovered from the shock of being told by his sons that Joseph was still alive and actually ruling over Egypt, that his רוּחַ 'lived' or 'came to life' (חיה√).[4] Similarly it is said of Samson, when he was faint with thirst after a particularly strenuous conflict with the Philistines, that, having succeeded by the aid of Yahweh in finding a spring and having drunk of its waters, 'his רוּחַ returned (שׁוב√), and he lived (חיה√)';[5] and, while we may not press the parallel too far, it is worthy of note that in English a similar situation might well be described in terms of the hero's recovery after being 'winded' in the struggle.

---

[1] Cf. 2 Kings ii. 9, 15.

[2] H. W. Robinson, *The Christian Experience of the Holy Spirit*, loc. cit., claims that in this connexion the original idea of רוּחַ was that of 'an invasive energy, used to explain the abnormal in man's conduct', but that in such passages as Judges xv. 19 and 1 Kings x. 5 (cited later in the text) it 'was so far naturalized as to allow the use of the term for the more marked energies of life, even when there was no suggestion of an invasion from the supernatural realm'. Cf. *The People and the Book*, p. 361; and see also Schoemaker, op. cit., pp. 18 f. It seems to the present writer that this is to go beyond the evidence; for the passages in question, although comparatively few, are as early as those which treat of the activity of the רוּחַ in terms of 'an invasion from the supernatural realm', so that there appears to be no justification for the view that the one conception was ever earlier than the other.

[3] See above, pp. 8 ff.   [4] Gen. xlv. 27 (E).

[5] Judges xv. 19: cf. 1 Sam. xxx. 12.

In much the same way the despondency shown by the
Queen of Sheba at Solomon's wisdom and style of living
is expressed by saying that 'there was no longer any רוּחַ
in her';[1] in other words, the situation was such that, as we
might say, she was not her usual 'breezy' self. Again, we
read of the Pharaoh that, when he awoke after dreaming of
the fat and lean kine and the rich and poor ears of corn,
'his רוּחַ was disturbed';[2] that is to say (if one may be per-
mitted the colloquialism), he quite properly and unmistakably 'had the wind up'! Finally, for example, we read that,
when Gideon soothed the angry feelings of the Ephraimites
by employing the proverbial 'soft answer' that 'turneth
away wrath',[3] their רוּחַ 'sank' (רפה√)[4]—just as we say of
a wind that it sinks or dies down. All in all, therefore, we
may say that in the early period (so far as our evidence goes)
a state of shock, or one of simple physical exhaustion, or
a despondent mood could each be regarded as offering a
clear indication of the absence of רוּחַ, whereas the behaviour
characteristic of human beings when they were in an agitated, angry, or (we may add) an obstinate mood[5] afforded
a corresponding indication of its presence. In short, amid
all the changing circumstances of life man's ordinary
physical powers were rightly felt to ebb and flow, just as
one's variable moods obviously come and go; and for the
Israelite all this might be expressed in terms of the presence
or absence of רוּחַ. At the same time we must not overlook
the fact that in this early period a display of ill feeling
might be described, not in terms of one's own רוּחַ, but in
terms of a רוּחַ רָעָה (EVV. 'evil spirit'), which had its
source in Yahweh;[6] and, what is more, any unusual manifestation of physical energy or mental alertness, such as

---

[1] 1 Kings x. 5 (= 2 Chron. ix. 4).
[2] Gen. xli. 8 (E).   [3] Prov. xv. 1.
[4] Judges viii. 3: cf. Eccles. x. 4 (of a man's 'mounting' anger). Cf., too,
the idiom whereby we speak in English of a 'gust of anger', or of a 'breeze'
which springs up between the parties to a quarrel.
[5] 1 Kings xxi. 5: cf. 1 Sam. i. 15 (but see LXX).
[6] Judges ix. 23: cf. 1 Sam. xvi. 14–23, xviii. 10, xix. 9.

the foresight of an administrator like Joseph,[1] the impulse
to action of the so-called 'judges',[2] or the oracular power
and extraordinary behaviour of the early prophets[3] (involving, perhaps, a temporary but complete change of character),[4] was normally attributed at this time to the personal
influence of the רוּחַ (as the 'Spirit') of Yahweh.[5]

In the circumstances it is not surprising that we should
find a form of polarization in the significance of the term
רוּחַ according as emphasis was laid upon the more sharply
physical or the more psychical aspects of life. In the former
case רוּחַ came to be used with a purely physical connotation
as a simple synonym for נְשָׁמָה, the ordinary word for
'breath'.[6] This use does not seem to have become at all
common before the Exile; but (even if we may rightly be
confident of our ability to arrange most of the extant records
in their historic sequence) the literary remains as a whole

---

[1] Gen. xli. 38 (E).

[2] Judges iii. 10, vi. 34, xi. 29, xiii. 25, xiv. 6, 19, xv. 14: cf. 1 Sam. xi. 6,
xvi. 13, 14; 1 Chron. xii. 19 (EVV. 18).

[3] Num. xi. 17, 24–30 (E), xxiv. 2 (J); 1 Sam. x. 5–13, xix. 18–24: cf. 2 Sam.
xxiii. 2. Cf., too, 1 Kings xviii. 12; 2 Kings ii. 16: and as regards 1 Kings
xxii. 21 ff. (= 2 Chron. xviii. 20 ff.), see *The One and the Many in the Israelite
Conception of God*, pp. 19 f., 2nd edit., pp. 15 f.

[4] Cf. 1 Sam. x. 6.

[5] It falls outside the scope of the present work to attempt to deal at all
fully with the conception of the רוּחַ as applied to Yahweh (or God); but, as is
pointed out above, p. 23, n. 1, the writer hopes to have an opportunity of
returning to this question in a subsequent publication. Meantime any reader
who may be interested is referred to the short study last cited (especially
pp. 17 ff., 2nd edit., pp. 13 ff.) for some indication of what the present writer
regards as the necessary line of approach.

[6] See above, p. 7, n. 4; and note incidentally the use of this term by synecdoche to indicate human beings of any kind: Deut. xx. 16; Joshua x. 40, xi.
11, 14; 1 Kings xv. 29; Ps. cl. 6; Isa. lvii. 16. Cf. E. König, *Stilistik, Rhetorik,
Poetik in Bezug auf die biblische Litteratur* (1900), pp. 57 ff. In N.H. it has
the developed meanings of 'spirit' or 'soul'. Cf. indeed for the shading off into
the former connotation Prov. xx. 27; also Job xxvi. 4, xxxii. 8. Note now
that T. C. Mitchell, 'The Old Testament Usage of *nešāmâ*', *V.T.* xi (1961),
pp. 177–87, rightly stresses the aforementioned use of נְשָׁמָה with reference
to human beings; but, despite his careful argument, I think that it is going
too far to suggest that this term is used in the Old Testament 'to denote the
breath of God, which, when imparted to man, made him unique among the
animals' (p. 186).

are so meagre that we must beware of saying that it was not known earlier. It is not inconceivable, for example, that we ought to say of the Queen of Sheba in connexion with the passage already discussed that, when she saw for herself Solomon's wisdom and splendour, it 'took her breath away'. In any case we may not overlook the fact that already in the J narrative of the Flood our word is used as a genitive along with נְשָׁמָה, in what appears to be a descriptive connexion, in order to refer to the animal creation as that which has breath (now further defined as a 'life-giving, wind-like breath')[1] in its nostrils, i.e. נִשְׁמַת רוּחַ חַיִּים;[2] and, while it is true that in this case the use of רוּחַ is commonly regarded as a harmonizing gloss,[3] such a suggestion needs to be received with caution in view of the fact that what appears to be a pre-exilic psalm offers another example of the same construction, which is used this time to define the breath of Yahweh either as 'His angry, wind-like breath' or as 'the wind-like breath of His Nostril', i.e. נִשְׁמַת רוּחַ אַפּוֹ.[4] This being the case, it would be an easy transition to go on to use the term רוּחַ as a substitute for נְשָׁמָה; so that we may well reserve judgement as to whether or not this practice came into being before the Exile, while recognizing that it was not uncommon from the Exile onwards. For example, an exilic poet, lamenting the overthrow of the Davidic

---

[1] Cf. Ezek. xxxvii. 1–14.

[2] Gen. vii. 22.

[3] e.g. H. Gunkel, H.K., 3rd edit. rev. (1910), S. R. Driver, W.C., 12th edit. enlarged (1926), J. Skinner, I.C.C. (1910), A. Clamer, S.B. (1953), *in loc.*

[4] 2 Sam. xxii. 16: cf. Ps. xviii. 16 (EVV. 15). For the pre-exilic date of this psalm, see the present writer's essay on 'The Rôle of the King in the Jerusalem Cultus', in *The Labyrinth: Further Studies in the Relation between Myth and Ritual in the Ancient World*, ed. S. H. Hooke (1935), pp. 71–111, esp. 100 ff.; and, better, the revision and development of the argument of the foregoing work which is now available in *Sacral Kingship in Ancient Israel* (1955), esp. pp. 107 ff. Cf., too, Exod. xv. 8 (J), where רוּחַ is used by itself to refer poetically to a wind as issuing from Yahweh's nostrils; and for the perpetuation of this poetical use of רוּחַ with reference to the wind as the 'breath' of God, see Job iv. 9 (נְשָׁמָה || רוּחַ אַפּוֹ); Isa. xl. 7, lix. 19; Hos. xiii. 15.

dynasty in Jerusalem, uses the term רוּחַ by itself in order to say of Zedekiah:[1]

> The breath (רוּחַ) of our nostrils, the Messiah of Yahweh,
>   Was caught in their pits;
> Of whom we said, 'In his shadow
>   We shall live (√חיה) amid the nations'.

Similarly the great prophet of the Exile employs the two terms under discussion as being practically synonymous, when he refers to Yahweh as the God—[2]

> Who created the heavens and stretched them out,
>   Who fashioned the earth and its products,
> Who giveth נְשָׁמָה to the people thereon,
>   And רוּחַ to those who walk therein.

In fact, this is the 'breath of life' (רוּחַ חַיִּים) which, according to the P code, is to be found 'in all flesh', and thus serves as the common characteristic which man shares with the whole of the animal world.[3] As such, of course, it is the gift of Yahweh, who is nothing if not the 'Giver of Life';[4] and in further illustration of this point we may cite Job, who employs the same terminology and similar parallelism in order to indicate that he still has energy enough to protest against the injustice which he is suffering, when he says:[5]

> For wholly, as yet, is my נְשָׁמָה in me,
>   Yea, the רוּחַ of God in my nostrils.

As a result Yahweh is to be contrasted with the idols on which men so often call; for these, however richly plated

---

[1] Lam. iv. 20: cf. Job ix. 18, xix. 17, xxxii. 18; Ps. cxlvi. 4; Isa. xi. 4, xxv. 4, xxxiii. 11. See also (of God) Ps. xxxiii. 6; Isa. xxx. 28, xxxiv. 16, xl. 7, lix. 19; Hos. xiii. 15. Finally, for the full significance of the term 'live' in the ensuing passage, see below, pp. 95 ff.; and for the importance attached to the king as such a 'breath of life' in respect of the social body, see the works cited in the previous note.

[2] Isa. xlii. 5. Cf. (of God) Job iv. 9; and for additional examples of this parallelism, see the passages from Job which are cited below, n. 5.

[3] Gen. vi. 17, vii. 15: cf. Ps. civ. 29, and especially Ezek. xxxvii. 1–10.

[4] See below, p. 106.

[5] Job xxvii. 3 (referred to above, p. 6, n. 2): cf. xxxiii. 4, xxxiv. 14 (and indeed xxxii. 8, as quoted below, p. 34). See also Ps. civ. 30.

with gold and silver, are lifeless and unresponsive, inasmuch as they obviously have no רוּחַ or 'breath'.[1]

The corresponding development in the use of the term רוּחַ (i.e. with an emphasis rather upon the psychical aspects of life) is much more colourful and interesting; but this is only to be expected. It is no more than a reasonable outcome of using this term in its secondary sense to denote the 'airy' or 'breezy' behaviour of any individual who is, as we say, 'full of life'. Beginning again with its emotional content, therefore, we have to note that, when a man's assurance fades away, this may be expressed in much the same way as of old by saying that רוּחַ no longer 'rises' in him,[2] or more simply that (as was the case with the Queen of Sheba) the person concerned is no longer in possession of any רוּחַ.[3] On the other hand, such despondency may be indicated equally well by saying of the רוּחַ that it grows dim,[4] becomes faint,[5] or vanishes.[6] Similarly, when it is necessary to indicate an agitated mood, one may continue to speak of the רוּחַ as being 'disturbed';[7] and indeed the term may always be employed to denote feelings of distress,[8] bitterness,[9] or anger.[10] At the same time, however, it should be noted that reference to the רוּחַ may indicate not merely a hot but also a cool temper,[11] a patient (or, more literally perhaps, a long-suffering) disposition as well as an impatient (or again, more literally perhaps, a short-tempered) one;[12] so

---

[1] Cf. Jer. x. 14 (= li. 17); Hab. ii. 19.

[2] Joshua ii. 11 (D).   [3] Joshua v. 1 (D).

[4] Isa. lxi. 3; Ezek. xxi. 12 (EVV. 7).

[5] Pss. lxxvii. 4 (EVV. 3), cxlii. 4 (EVV. 3), cxliii. 4: cf. Isa. lvii. 16.

[6] Ps. cxliii. 7.

[7] Dan. ii. 3: see above, p. 26, n. 2.

[8] Job vi. 4, vii. 11; Prov. xv. 4, 13, xvii. 22, xviii. 14; Isa. liv. 6, lxv. 14: cf. Pss. xxxiv. 19 (EVV. 18), li. 19 (EVV. 17); Isa. lxvi. 2; also (of God) Isa. lxiii. 10.

[9] Gen. xxvi. 35 (P); Ps. cvi. 33, reading הָמְרוּ for הִמְרוּ (cf., for example, H. Gunkel, H.K. (1926), *in loc.*).

[10] Job xv. 13; Prov. xxix. 11; Eccles. x. 4: also (of God) Zech. vi. 8.

[11] Cf. (*a*) Ezek. iii. 14; also Eccles. vii. 9 (of a hasty temper): (*b*) Prov. xvii. 27.

[12] Cf. (*a*) Eccles. vii. 8; also Prov. xviii. 14: (*b*) Exod. vi. 9 (P); Job xxi. 4; Prov. xiv. 29; also (of God) Mic. ii. 7.

that to 'rule over' one's רוּחַ is the proverbial and obvious way of showing real self-control.[1]

Nevertheless the vagaries of the רוּחַ, *qua* 'wind', also made it the obvious term for denoting almost any mood, disposition, or frame of mind (as we say); and indeed it seems to have been possible to resort to it as a means of expressing the whole range of man's emotional, intellectual, and volitional life.[2] Most of the evidence for this development appears to come from the exilic and post-exilic age; but again we must beware of over-emphasizing this point. With so little material at our disposal and with the dating of some passages still in dispute, we shall do well to leave it an open question as to whether or not there was any considerable movement in this direction during the pre-exilic period.[3] So far as the development itself is concerned, an outstanding feature is that whereby, instead of speaking in terms of a man's own רוּחַ, one speaks rather of a particular type of רוּחַ, suitably defined by a following noun in the genitive and apparently operating as an extraneous influence, the origin of which is sometimes ascribed to Yahweh and sometimes left unindicated. Thus Isaiah (it seems) can think of Yahweh as reducing the citizens of Jerusalem to a state of coma by 'pouring out' upon them 'a רוּחַ of deep sleep',[4] while Hosea speaks of Israel's proneness to apostasy as being due to 'a רוּחַ of whoredom'[5] (corresponding to the 'רוּחַ of uncleanness', to which a post-exilic prophet refers);[6] and in much the same way the P code legislates for the procedure to be adopted when 'a רוּחַ of jealousy' is found to 'come over' a man, so that he grows suspicious of his wife.[7] Similarly (but with an emphasis now upon the higher level represented by the more intellectual aspect of man's psychical life), when Egypt is threatened with civil war, this is not only ascribed to the

---

[1] Prov. xvi. 32, xxv. 28.

[2] Cf. the way in which (with an echo of the Latin *spiritus*) we speak of one's 'spiritual' life as distinct from mere 'spirited' behaviour.

[3] Cf. Jean, op. cit., p. 119. [4] Isa. xxix. 10.

[5] iv. 12, v. 4. [6] Zech. xiii. 2. [7] Num. v. 14, 30.

fact that Egypt's own רוּחַ will have been 'emptied out', i.e. that it will have lost its wits or become devoid of all reason;[1] but the prophet who paints this scene goes on to complete the picture by mocking Egypt's political leaders for having created this situation through their own warped judgement, because Yahweh Himself has introduced 'a רוּחַ of distortion' into the national life.[2] This corresponds to the thought that the justice which is to be characteristic of the new era, ushered in by the Day of Yahweh, will be due to the fact that Yahweh Himself will then ensure that there is 'a רוּחַ of justice' in those who are called upon to administer the law;[3] and in a similar way the able administrator,[4] like the skilled craftsman,[5] is said to be 'filled' (and in the latter case 'filled' by Yahweh) with 'a רוּחַ of wisdom'.

It is in line with the foregoing (and indeed with the practice of the earlier period) that these more psychical powers should sometimes be attributed directly to the רוּחַ of Yahweh, who, as being 'רוּחַ and not flesh',[6] is the author and sustainer of 'the רוּחַ of all flesh'[7]—conceivable as 'hovering' over the cosmic waters at the creation of the world[8] and ever able in this extended fashion to make His

---

[1] Isa. xix. 3: cf. xxix. 24.

[2] Verse 14. Cf. (*a*) the רוּחַ שֶׁקֶר of 1 Kings xxii. 22 f. (= 2 Chron. xviii. 21 f.) with Mic. ii. 11: (*b*) 2 Kings xix. 7 (= Isa. xxxvii. 7): and for an introduction to the question as to how an Israelite would think of the personal influence of Yahweh (direct or indirect) in such a connexion, see above, p. 27, n. 3, *ad fin.*

[3] Isa. xxviii. 6: cf. (of Yahweh) Isa. iv. 4.

[4] Deut. xxxiv. 9 (P): cf. Num. xxvii. 18 (P).

[5] Exod. xxviii. 3 (P): cf. 1 Chron. xxviii. 12.

[6] Cf. the implication of Isa. xxxi. 3; also, perhaps, Gen. vi. 3 (J): and see again *The One and the Many in the Israelite Conception of God*, pp. 17 ff., 2nd edit., pp. 13 ff.

[7] Cf., in addition to the many appropriate passages already cited, Num. xvi. 22, xxvii. 16 (both P); Job x. 12 (in contrast with xvii. 1), xii. 10; Ps. xxxi. 6 (EVV. 5); Ezek. xxxvii. 14; Eccles. iii. 19 and 21, in conjunction with xii. 7; Zech. xii. 1.

[8] Gen. i. 2 (P). This is to reject the view that רוּחַ here has the meaning 'wind', and that the ensuing reference to 'God' should be regarded as an example of the use of אֱלֹהִים with a superlative force which is discussed, for example, by D. W. Thomas, op. cit., pp. 213 ff., so that the whole expression

influence felt in the affairs of mankind.[1] Thus we find that

is construed with the *Pi'ēl* participle of √רחף as referring, not to any impending influence of the divine 'Spirit', but to the movement of 'a great wind'. This interpretation has a long history, as may be seen from the important article by K. Smoronski, ' "Et spiritus Dei ferebatur super aquas." Inquisitio historico-exegetica in interpretationem textus Gen. 1, 2c', *Biblica* vi (1925), pp. 140–56, 275–93, 361–95: and of recent years it has often been advanced afresh, e.g. by L. Waterman, 'Cosmogonic Affinities in Genesis 1:2', *A.J.S.L.* xliii (1926–7), pp. 177–84; J. M. P. Smith, 'The Syntax and Meaning of Genesis 1:1–3', *A.J.S.L.* xliv (1927–8), pp. 108–15 (cf. the symposium *Old Testament Essays*, with a foreword by D. C. Simpson (1927), pp. 163–71), also 'The Use of Divine Names as Superlatives', *A.J.S.L.* xlv (1928–9), pp. 212 f.; K. Galling, 'Der Charakter der Chaosschilderung in Gen. 1, 2', *Z.T.K.* xlvii (1950), pp. 145–57; H. M. Orlinsky, 'The Plain Meaning of *Ruaḥ* in Gen. 1. 2', *J.Q.R.* xlviii (1957–8), pp. 174–82; N. H. Ridderbos, 'Genesis i 1 und 2', *O.T.S.* xii (1958), pp. 241 ff.; Scheepers, op. cit., pp. 246 ff. Cf., too, T. J. Meek, in *The Bible: An American Translation*, ed. J. M. P. Smith and E. J. Goodspeed (1935), *in loc.*; and G. von Rad, A.T.D., 6th edit. (1961), pp. 37 f., E.T. by J. H. Marks (1961), pp. 47 f. After being attracted by this view for some years I am now convinced that it is fundamentally wrong. The verb רחף, which is used here in the *Pi'ēl*, is rare; but its meaning is clear enough. It is found once in the *Qal* with the force of 'fluttering' or 'quivering'; i.e. in Jer. xxiii. 9, of the bones of a man who is in anguish of heart under the impact of Yahweh's words. The *Pi'ēl* is found once elsewhere, again with the basic idea of 'fluttering' but, in this case, with the implication of 'hovering'; i.e. in Deut. xxxii. 11, of an eagle which is poised for action above its young. The same meaning is also required for the cognate Ugaritic √rḥp as found in Gordon, *Ugaritic Manual*, ii, 1 Aqht: 32; 3 Aqht: 20, 21, 31, or, better, Driver, *Canaanite Myths and Legends*, A III i 20, 21, 31, 32, i.e. of Anat's joining the eagles to hover over Aqhat; and it is significant that here again, as in Deut. xxxii. 11, the verb is used in a context which implies the thought of hovering with a definite purpose in view. Further, so far as the term רוּחַ itself is concerned, one should beware of divorcing the thought of God's creative word from that of the invasive activity of His רוּחַ qua 'Spirit' (cf., for example, 2 Sam. xxiii. 2 f.; Zech. vii. 12); so that it is quite misleading to suggest that an allusion to the divine 'Spirit' in the verse under discussion has no bearing on the sequel with its recurrent reference to the divine *fiat*. However, the whole question needs to be examined in a wider context than is possible here, and I hope to return to it in the work which is referred to above, p. 23, n. 1, *ad fin.*

[1] Cf. (in addition to the passages already cited in connexion with pp. 26 f. and those still to be cited in connexion with the ensuing discussion) Pss. cxxxix. 7, cxliii. 10; Isa. xliv. 3, lxiii. 11, 14; Ezek. i. 12, 20, 21, x. 17; Hag. ii. 4 f.: and for the part thus played by the רוּחַ in extension of the personality of the Godhead, see again *The One and the Many in the Israelite Conception of God*. Incidentally it is a failure to give due weight to this distinction between Yahweh as the Godhead and the 'extensions' of His personality which has led to the complete misrepresentation of the writer's point of view by Brockington, op. cit., p. 9, n. 2.

a prophet can still think (or be thought of) in terms of his traditional connexion with the רוּחַ of Yahweh,[1] and so can look forward to the time when God will 'pour out' His רוּחַ upon 'all flesh'.[2] Moreover, when the רוּחַ thus 'falls' or 'alights' upon an individual,[3] it may be that this will 'enter in'[4] and take possession of him in such a manner as to let him feel that he is in the grip (literally 'the Hand')[5] of God and capable of being 'carried away' in an experience which is unmistakably ecstatic.[6] On the other hand, an experience of this kind is by no means the only or necessary consequence of being subject to possession by the רוּחַ of Yahweh. It may issue, rather, in those temperate qualities which characterize the ideal servant of Yahweh and specifically His vicegerent upon earth, of whom the prophet says:[7]

> There shall rest upon him the רוּחַ of Yahweh,
> A רוּחַ of wisdom and discernment,
> A רוּחַ of counsel and might,
> A רוּחַ of knowledge and the fear of Yahweh.

Nor is this all. It may even manifest itself in the quiet skill of the craftsman[8] or, indeed, the simple intelligence of an ordinary individual; for,[9]

> Of a surety, it is רוּחַ in man
> And the breath (נְשָׁמָה) of Shaddai,[10] that giveth them understanding.

---

[1] 2 Chron. xv. 1, xx. 14, xxiv. 20; Neh. ix. 30; Hos. ix. 7; Mic. iii. 8; Zech. vii. 12: cf. Isa. xlviii. 16, lix. 21, lxi. 1.

[2] Joel iii. 1–2 (EVV. ii. 28–29): cf. Isa. xxxii. 15; Ezek. xxxvi. 27, xxxix. 29.

[3] Cf. Ezek. xi. 5: and, for the force of the verb, see perhaps Gen. xxiv. 64 (J), 2 Kings v. 21.

[4] Cf. Ezek. ii. 2, iii. 24.

[5] Cf. Ezek. iii. 14, viii. 3, xxxvii. 1: and see further on this point F. Haeussermann, *Wortempfang und Symbol in der alttestamentlichen Prophetie*, B.Z.A.W. 58 (1932), pp. 22–24.

[6] Cf. Ezek. iii. 12, 14, viii. 3, xi. 1, 24, xxxvii. 1, xliii. 5: and for the phenomena of 'possession' and 'ecstasy' in this connexion, see *The Cultic Prophet in Ancient Israel*, p. 19, n. 6, 2nd edit., p. 18, n. 4.

[7] Isa. xi. 2: cf. xlii. 1 ff.; Zech. iv. 6.

[8] Exod. xxxi. 3, xxxv. 31 (both P): cf. p. 32, n. 5.

[9] Job xxxii. 8: cf. xx. 3; also Neh. ix. 20.

[10] EVV., R.S.V.: 'the Almighty'.

In short, it appears that king and commoner are alike dependent upon the רוּחַ of Yahweh; and this dependence involves not only their simple, physical existence but also the very potentialities of their psychical life.

However, it is in one's own essential רוּחַ (with all that this involves in the grasping of a totality and the exercise of self-control)[1] that the forceful and indeed purposeful individual is revealed. The thoughts which men thus admit (i.e. מַעֲלוֹת רוּחָם, as Ezekiel would say)[2] are normally directed to a particular end,[3] although it is recognized that even at his best the individual may not be so aware of his motives as Yahweh, who is able to assess every man's רוּחַ.[4] On the other hand, the incentive to action may be said to come from Yahweh Himself, as when the Deuteronomist makes Moses say of Sihon's obstinacy in refusing the Israelites a safe passage through his territory that Yahweh had 'hardened' his רוּחַ.[5] Similarly we are told on more than one occasion that Yahweh 'roused' the רוּחַ of a foreign ruler or people to engage in war,[6] just as He is said to have 'roused' the רוּחַ of Cyrus (as well as that of certain Jewish exiles) to undertake the rebuilding of the Temple;[7] and *mutatis mutandis* this corresponds to the statement of P that offerings were brought for the building of the Tabernacle by every man whose רוּחַ 'made him willing'.[8] In short, it is through the activity of the רוּחַ, actuated as this may be by faithful[9] or deceitful[10] motives, that the will of man finds its expression; and while a study of the Old

---

[1] See above, p. 31, n. 1.

[2] xi. 5: cf. xx. 32. Cf., too, the corresponding idiom in the case of the heart, as noticed below, p. 78, n. 2.

[3] Cf. Ps. lxxvii. 7 (EVV. 6); Prov. i. 23, xvi. 2; Isa. xxvi. 9; Ezek. xi. 5, xiii. 3, xx. 32; Mal. ii. 15, 16: also (of God) Isa. xxx. 1.

[4] Prov. xvi. 2: cf. (of God) Isa. xl. 13.

[5] Deut. ii. 30: cf. the 'hardening' of the heart, as noted below, p. 80, n. 3.

[6] 1 Chron. v. 26; 2 Chron. xxi. 16; Jer. li. 11 (cf. verse 1): cf. Ps. lxxvi. 13 (EVV. 12).

[7] 2 Chron. xxxvi. 22 (= Ezra i. 1); Ezra i. 5: cf. Hag. i. 14.

[8] Exod. xxxv. 21 (P).

[9] Ps. lxxviii. 8; Prov. xi. 13: cf. Num. xiv. 24 (JE).

[10] Cf. Ps. xxxii. 2.

Testament reveals that it was often a matter of dispute as
to how Yahweh's will was to be defined, the ideal for the
devout Israelite was that his own רוּחַ should be in accord
with that of Yahweh, i.e.:[1]

> Create for me a clean heart, O God,
>   And make new within me a steadfast רוּחַ.
> Do not cast me out from Thy presence
>   By taking Thy holy רוּחַ from me.
> Let me enjoy Thy salvation once again,
>   Supported by Thee with a willing רוּחַ.

For the Israelite this would be the prayer of one on whom
Yahweh had poured 'a רוּחַ of grace and of supplication'
(if we may follow the rendering of the Revised Version),[2]
inasmuch as the speaker has come before Him with 'a
broken רוּחַ', i.e. no longer self-willed.[3] It reflects that 'lowliness',[4] rather than 'loftiness',[5] of רוּחַ which is necessary
(according to the religious teachers of Israel), if one is to
find favour with Yahweh; for[6]

> Thus saith the high and exalted One,
>   That abideth for ever, whose Name is holy:
> 'On high and in holiness I dwell,
>   But also with the contrite and the lowly in רוּחַ;
> Bringing life to the רוּחַ of the lowly,
>   Bringing life to the heart of the contrite.'

Finally in this connexion, it should be noted that, when the
prophet lets Yahweh speak in this way of 'bringing life' or
'giving life' (√חיה)[7] to the רוּחַ of the lowly and the heart of

---

[1] Ps. li. 12–14 (EVV. 10–12): cf. Ezek. xi. 19 f., xviii. 31, xxxvi. 26 (and
note xxxvi. 27, xxxvii. 14). In the passage quoted it is possible and even
probable that, as the term under discussion is usually feminine, verse 12b
should be rendered literally as 'Make new within me *the* רוּחַ *of a steadfast
man*'. Cf. verse 19, where it is clearly construed as a feminine noun; and see
further G. R. Driver, in *J.R.A.S.* (1948), p. 175, n. 2.

[2] Cf. Zech. xii. 10.

[3] Verse 19 (EVV. 17): cf. the 'hardening' of the רוּחַ referred to above,
p. 35, n. 5.

[4] Prov. xvi. 19, xxix. 23; Isa. lvii. 15.

[5] Prov. xvi. 18; Eccles. vii. 8.

[6] Isa. lvii. 15. For the thought, cf. Ps. xxxiv. 19 (EVV. 18); Isa. lxvi. 2:
for the language, cf. Isa. xxxviii. 16.   [7] EVV. 'to revive'.

the contrite, the thought is wholly in line with the fact that, as already observed, Yahweh, who is the author and sustainer of man's being in both the narrowly physical and the more broadly psychical sense, is nothing if not the 'Giver of Life'.[1]

III

The conception of man as a psycho-physical organism may be seen equally clearly when one examines the use of the terminology for the various parts of the body;[2] for, besides being referred to in a simple, straightforward way as mere instruments of the *ego* (אֲנִי or אָנֹכִי), they are sometimes spoken of as themselves actively engaged in some form of personal behaviour or as characterized by some personal quality. This is even true to a slight degree of the flesh (שְׁאֵר, בָּשָׂר),[3] which incidentally is often referred to in such a way as to mark man off as belonging to a different order of being from that of God,[4] and is sometimes clearly used by synecdoche (*pars pro toto*) for the body itself, e.g.:[5]

And it came to pass, when Ahab heard these words, that he rent his clothes, and put sackcloth upon his flesh, and fasted.

[1] See below, pp. 106 ff.

[2] Cf. in general the works of Koeberle, H. W. Robinson, Dhorme, Pedersen, and Eichrodt, which are cited above, p. 4, n. 1; also Burton, *Spirit, Soul, and Flesh*, pp. 68 ff.: but note that here again the ensuing discussion is based upon an independent examination of all the instances of the use of each term under consideration. It should also be observed that the writer is not concerned to deal with all the parts of the body, but only with those which throw light upon the principle under discussion.

[3] On the distinction between these two terms, see Dhorme, op. cit., pp. 7 ff.

[4] Cf. Gen. vi. 3 (J); 2 Chron. xxxii. 8; Job xii. 10; Pss. lvi. 5 (EVV. 4), lxv. 3 (EVV. 2), lxxviii. 39, cxlv. 21; Isa. xxxi. 3, xl. 6 ff., xlix. 26, lxvi. 16, 23 f.; Jer. xii. 12, xvii. 5, xxv. 31, xxxii. 27, xlv. 5; Ezek. xxi. 4 (EVV. xx. 28), xxi. 9 f. (EVV. 4 f.); Joel iii. 1 (EVV. ii. 28); Zech. ii. 17 (EVV. 13).

[5] 1 Kings xxi. 27: cf. Lev. xiii. 38 (P), xvii. 15 f. (H); Num. viii. 7 (P); 2 Kings vi. 30; Job iv. 15; Prov. iv. 22, &c.: also (with גֶּלֶד) Job xvi. 15; and (with עוֹר) Exod. xxii. 26 (EVV. 27). See further König, *Stilistik, Rhetorik, Poetik in Bezug auf die biblische Litteratur*, pp. 59 f.; also Burton, op. cit., p. 69. Cf., too, Dhorme, op. cit., p. 9, apropos Lev. xviii. 6, xxv. 49 (both H).

Such a use is deserving of notice, for examples of this kind add force to those passages in which the flesh is clearly associated with psychical functions, as when the psalmist says:[1]

> How lovely the place where Thou dost dwell,
>   Yahweh of Hosts!
> My whole being (נֶפֶשׁ) longeth, yea pineth,[2]
>   For Yahweh's courts;
> My heart and my flesh (בָּשָׂר) acclaim
>   The Living God.

Indeed the parallelism with נֶפֶשׁ is occasionally so marked that the use of the term for 'flesh' almost approaches the common use of the former term as a periphrasis for the personal pronoun (such as may be seen, in fact, in the foregoing passage); for example, to quote another psalmist:[3]

> Yahweh,[4] Thou art my God! Thee do I seek!
> My whole being (נֶפֶשׁ) thirsteth for Thee.[5]
> My flesh (בָּשָׂר) fainteth for Thee, a very land in drought,[6]
>   Exhausted for lack of water.

An equally good example is afforded by the aphorism which is rendered in the English Versions as:[7]

> The merciful man doeth good to his own soul (נֶפֶשׁ);
>   But he that is cruel troubleth his own flesh (שְׁאֵר).

In principle, however, this is simply the Israelite way of saying (in the words of a modern American translation):[8]

> A kindly man does good to himself;
>   But a cruel man does harm to himself.

---

[1] Ps. lxxxiv. 2 f. (EVV. 1 f.): cf. Job iv. 15, xxi. 6; Pss. xvi. 9, cxix. 120; Eccles. ii. 3, v. 5 (EVV. 6), xi. 10; also Ps. lxxiii. 26.

[2] Or simply, 'I long, yea pine': see above, pp. 15 ff.

[3] Ps. lxiii. 2 (EVV. 1). Cf., in addition to the example which follows in the text, Job xiii. 14, xiv. 22; also, in general, Ps. xxvii. 2; Prov. iv. 22, xiv. 30.

[4] M.T. 'God'.

[5] Or simply, 'I thirst for Thee': cf. n. 2.

[6] i.e. an example of the *bêth essentiae* (G.K., § 119i).

[7] Prov. xi. 17.

[8] i.e. by A. R. Gordon, in *The Bible: An American Translation*, ed. J. M. P. Smith and E. J. Goodspeed (as cited above, p. 32, n. 8): cf. C. H. Toy, I.C.C. (1899), *in loc.*; and see now R.S.V.

The Hebrew terms involved are here practically synonymous; the variation is merely due to the antithetic parallelism which the author has introduced into his couplet, and
the term under discussion is simply used by synecdoche for
a man's person or self as a whole. Accordingly we must
beware of the suggestion that such language reveals a belief
in what has been described as 'the diffusion of consciousness'.[1]

The head (רֹאשׁ) offers little occasion for comment; for,
in so far as it becomes the focus of attention, this tends to
be concentrated rather upon one or another of its distinctive
parts, i.e. the face, the eyes, the ears, and so on. Nevertheless, we may note in passing that mockery or derision might
be expressed by the shaking of the head,[2] while the bowed
head must have been recognized quite early as a sign of
weakness or humiliation.[3] Moreover, just as blessing might
be bestowed by laying one's hand upon the head of the
recipient,[4] so the responsibility for shed blood or trouble
of any kind could be spoken of in terms of its descending or
recoiling upon one's head;[5] and we may recall the way in
which Achish of Gath expressed his confidence in David by
saying, 'I will make thee a keeper of my head', i.e. as we
should say, 'a guardian of my person' or 'one of my body-
guard'.[6] Indeed, as in English, one might employ such
obvious synecdoche to indicate distribution 'per head',[7]
although in the later literature such singling out of the

---

[1] Cf. H. W. Robinson, followed by L. H. Brockington, as referred to below,
p. 81, n. 5.

[2] Cf. (a) 2 Kings xix. 21 (= Isa. xxxvii. 22); Job xvi. 4; Pss. xxii. 8 (EVV.
7), cix. 25; Lam. ii. 15: (b) Ps. xliv. 15 (EVV. 14); Jer. xviii. 16.

[3] Cf. Lam. ii. 10 with the idiomatic language of (a) Gen. xl. 13, 20 (E);
2 Kings xxv. 27 (= Jer. lii. 31); Job x. 15; Ps. lxxxiii. 3 (EVV. 2); Zech.¹ i.
4 (EVV. i. 21): (b) Pss. iii. 4 (EVV. 3), xxvii. 6, cx. 7.

[4] Gen. xlviii. 13 ff. (E): cf. Gen. xlix. 26; Deut. xxxiii. 16; Prov. x. 6, xi. 26.

[5] Cf. (a) Joshua ii. 19; 2 Sam. i. 16, iii. 29; 1 Kings ii. 32, 33, 37; Ezek.
xxxiii. 4: (b) Judges ix. 57; 1 Sam. xxv. 39; 1 Kings ii. 44, viii. 32 (= 2 Chron.
vi. 23); Neh. iii. 36 (EVV. iv. 4); Esther ix. 25; Ps. vii. 17 (EVV. 16); Ezek.
ix. 10, xi. 21, xvi. 43, xvii. 19, xxii. 31; Joel iv. 4, 7 (EVV. iii. 4, 7); Obad. 15:
also (c) Prov. xxv. 22; Jer. xxiii. 19, xxx. 23.

[6] 1 Sam. xxviii. 2.   [7] Judges v. 30.

40 *The Vitality of the Individual*

individual[1] is normally expressed by reference to the 'skull' or, more appropriately if somewhat archaically, the 'poll' (גֻּלְגֹּלֶת);[2] and we may compare the way in which death in one's old age is sometimes indicated by speaking of the time when one's 'grey hair' (שֵׂיבָה) will descend to Sheol.[3] In each of these cases the presence of synecdoche with its implicit grasping of a totality is clear enough, and needs no further elaboration.

However, a much more interesting term in many ways is that for 'face' (פָּנִים); and this, no doubt, has its source in the fact that the face was found to be extraordinarily revealing in respect of man's various emotions, moods, and dispositions, as when we read:[4]

And Jacob saw the face of Laban, and, behold, it was not friendly towards him (*lit.* with him) as formerly.

Indeed the fact that in Hebrew the use of this common Semitic noun is restricted to the plural form is sufficient to indicate the importance which was attached to what we should call one's 'features'.[5] Thus for the Israelite the face may reveal a grim determination which makes it comparable with flint,[6] and it may harden correspondingly into an expression which foreshadows defiant,[7] impudent,[8] or even ruthless[9] behaviour, and so may suggest a fierceness like that of the lion.[10] Similarly what we should call a 'beaming'

---

[1] Cf. now in part E. A. Speiser, 'Census and Ritual Expiation in Mari and Israel', *B.A.S.O.R.* 149 (February 1958), pp. 17–25, esp. 20 ff., with reference to the use of נָשָׂא אֶת־רֹאשׁ וגו׳ in (*a*) Gen. xl. 20 (E), and (*b*) such passages as Exod. xxx. 12, Num. i. 2, iv. 2, xxvi. 2, xxxi. 26 (all P).

[2] Exod. xvi. 16 (P), xxxviii. 26 (P); Num. i. 2, 18, 20, 22, iii. 47 (all P); 1 Chron. xxiii. 3, 24.

[3] Gen. xlii. 38, xliv. 29, 31 (all J); 1 Kings ii. 6, 9: cf. Lev. xix. 32 (H); Ruth iv. 15.

[4] Gen. xxxi. 2: cf. verse 5 (both E).

[5] Cf. Dhorme, *L'Emploi métaphorique, &c.*, pp. 42 f.

[6] Isa. l. 7: cf. Ezek. iii. 8.

[7] Jer. v. 3; Ezek. ii. 4.

[8] Prov. vii. 13, xxi. 29: cf. Eccles. viii. 1b.

[9] Deut. xxviii. 50; Dan. viii. 23.

[10] 1 Chron. xii. 9 (EVV. 8).

face reveals a cheerful[1] or kindly[2] mood, while a change of colour or the like may betoken humiliation,[3] fear,[4] anguish,[5] or some corresponding form of distress.[6] In the same way, whereas the awareness of one's innocence in any matter enables a man to 'raise' or 'hold up' his face,[7] a downcast (*lit.* 'fallen') face is a clear indication of anger.[8] Accordingly it is not surprising that one should speak of making a person's face 'sweet' (i.e. as opposed to its having what we should call a 'bitter' or a 'sour' look) in an effort to conciliate him or obtain his favour, although in this case we have an idiom which is so well established and, what is more, one which is so commonly used in quite a formal way with reference to Yahweh, that we must beware of laying too great a stress upon its literal meaning.[9] Similarly the 'hiding'

---

[1] Job xxix. 24: cf. Prov. xv. 13.

[2] Prov. xvi. 15; Eccles. viii. 1a. Cf. (of God) Num. vi. 25 (P); Pss. iv. 7 (EVV. 6), xxxi. 17 (EVV. 16), xliv. 4 (EVV. 3), lxvii. 2 (EVV. 1), lxxx. 4, 8, 20 (EVV. 3, 7, 19), lxxxix. 16 (EVV. 15), cxix. 135; Dan. ix. 17: but bear in mind that in these cases the obviously formal language may have been influenced by the cultic association of Yahweh with the sun. Cf. Ps. xc. 8 with the foregoing passages; and see below, pp. 106 ff., i.e. with reference to Yahweh as the Lord of light and life. Cf., too, the argument of the writer's essay 'The Rôle of the King in the Jerusalem Cultus' and, better, that of *Sacral Kingship in Ancient Israel* (as cited above, p. 28, n. 4).

[3] 2 Sam. xix. 6 (EVV. 5); 2 Chron. xxxii. 21; Ezra ix. 7; Pss. xxxiv. 6 (EVV. 5), xliv. 16 (EVV. 15), lxix. 8 (EVV. 7), lxxxiii. 17 (EVV. 16); Isa. xxix. 22; Jer. vii. 19, li. 51; Ezek. vii. 18; Dan. ix. 7, 8. Cf. the English expression 'shamefaced'.

[4] Isa. xiii. 8; Ezek. xxvii. 35; Joel ii. 6; Nahum ii. 11 (EVV. 10).

[5] Jer. xxx. 6.

[6] Gen. xl. 7 (E); Neh. ii. 2, 3; Job xvi. 16; Eccles. vii. 3: cf. Dan. i. 10. See also 1 Sam. i. 18 and Job ix. 27, which have something of a parallel in the English idiom 'to make a face'.

[7] 2 Sam. ii. 22; Job xi. 15, xxii. 26.

[8] Gen. iv. 5, 6 (J): cf. (of God) Jer. iii. 12. Cf. Prov. xxv. 23; also (of God) Ps. lxxx. 17 (EVV. 16).

[9] (*a*) i.e. *conciliation*: only of God, Exod. xxxii. 11 (JE); 1 Kings xiii. 6; 2 Kings xiii. 4; 2 Chron. xxxiii. 12; Jer. xxvi. 19; Dan. ix. 13; Mal. i. 9: (*b*) i.e. *entreating favour*: of man, Job xi. 19; Ps. xlv. 13 (EVV. 12); Prov. xix. 6: of God, 1 Sam. xiii. 12; Ps. cxix. 58; Zech. vii. 2, viii. 21, 22. Cf. Gen. xxxii. 21 (EVV. 20) (J). The reader should note, however, that the etymology adopted here is a matter of dispute. Cf., for example, K.B., s.v. I חלה, as against B.D.B., s.v. II חלה.

of one's face,[1] somewhat like the turning of one's back,[2] affords a graphic picture of aversion or displeasure; and both of these expressions have an obvious parallel in the equally idiomatic 'turning back' of someone else's face as a mark of disapproval.[3] On the other hand, to 'raise' another person's face, an idiom which suggests an origin in the attitude of a suppliant, is a picturesque indication of favour or respect[4] (and even favouritism or partiality)[5] with consequent social standing as a person of distinction.[6]

Nevertheless here again we must beware of laying too great a stress upon what have obviously become mere figures of speech; for, as in the case of the prepositional phrases derived from this source,[7] it is probable that the original significance of the Hebrew was hardly felt. The fact is that in these cases we are approaching the secondary use of the term פָּנִים, which has arisen through the employment of synecdoche. Thus the fact that the various expressions for the 'fixing' or 'turning' of the face in a particular direction normally serve as an obvious indication of purpose or intention, and thus point to the concentration of the נֶפֶשׁ (or the personality as a whole) upon the end in view, means that in many, if not most, of these cases the use of the Hebrew term under discussion does not fall far short of making it a parallel to the latter term, when this is used

---

[1] Isa. l. 6, liii. 3: also (of God) Deut. xxxi. 17 f.; Job xiii. 24; Pss. xiii. 2 (EVV. 1), xxvii. 9, li. 11 (EVV. 9); Isa. liv. 8, lxiv. 6 (EVV. 7); Jer. xxxiii. 5; Ezek. xxxix. 23 f., and so often. Cf. Ezek. xiv. 6; also 1 Kings xxi. 4; 2 Chron. xxix. 6: and (of God) Ezek. vii. 22.

[2] Cf. 2 Chron. xxix. 6; Jer. ii. 27, xxxii. 33.

[3] 1 Kings ii. 16, 17, 20; 2 Kings xviii. 24 (= Isa. xxxvi. 9); 2 Chron. vi. 42; Ps. cxxxii. 10. Contrast Ps. lxxxiv. 10 (EVV. 9).

[4] Gen. xix. 21 (J), xxxii. 21 (EVV. 20) (J); Deut. xxviii. 50; 1 Sam. xxv. 35; 2 Kings iii. 14; Job xlii. 8 f.; Lam. iv. 16b; Mal. i. 8 f.: cf. Lev. xix. 32 (H); Lam. v. 12.

[5] Lev. xix. 15 (H); Deut. x. 17; Job xiii. 8, 10, xxxii. 21, xxxiv. 19; Ps. lxxxii. 2; Prov. xviii. 5; Mal. ii. 9. Cf. 2 Chron. xix. 7; Prov. vi. 35 (!): also the corresponding idiom in Deut. i. 17, xvi. 19; Prov. xxiv. 23, xxviii. 21; Isa. iii. 9.

[6] i.e. in the expression נְשׂוּא פָנִים: 2 Kings v. 1; Job xxii. 8; Isa. iii. 3, ix. 14.

[7] i.e. מִפְּנֵי, לִפְנֵי, &c.

either as a simple reflexive or as a periphrasis for the personal pronoun.[1] For example, when the Chronicler says of Jehoshaphat that 'he set his face to seek Yahweh', this is simply the Hebrew way of saying that 'he set himself to seek Yahweh' (cf. EVV.);[2] and when he says of Sennacherib that 'his face was for war against Jerusalem', this obviously means that he intended (EVV. 'he purposed') to fight against Jerusalem or, as we say, that 'he was out for war against Jerusalem'.[3] Similarly the common idiom 'to see so-and-so's face', which corresponds to the much rarer idiom of seeing a person 'face to face',[4] is used quite simply and with a perceptible weakening of its literal meaning to denote the enjoyment of personal contact with someone else (especially one's social superior); so that, when used with a suffix, as frequently happens, it serves as a simple periphrasis for the personal pronoun: e.g. 'to see my face' is really no more than an emphatic way of saying 'to see me'.[5]

---

[1] Cf. in general (*a*) Gen. xxxi. 21 (E); 1 Kings ii. 15; 2 Kings xii. 18; Jer. xlii. 15; Ezek. vi. 2, and so often; similarly (of God) Jer. xxi. 10, &c.: (*b*) 2 Chron. xx. 3; Dan. ix. 3; similarly (of God) Lev. xvii. 10 (H), &c.: (*c*) 2 Kings ix. 32; similarly (of God) Num. vi. 26 (P): (*d*) Jer. ii. 27, xxxii. 33: (*e*) the following sporadic examples, Exod. x. 10 (J); Num. xxiv. 1 (J); 2 Kings viii. 11; 2 Chron. xxxii. 2; Ezra ix. 6; Jer. l. 5; Ezek. iv. 3, 7; Dan. xi. 19 (cf. 17 f.); and (of God) Ps. xxxiv. 17 (EVV. 16). Cf., too, Judges xviii. 23; 1 Kings viii. 14 (= 2 Chron. vi. 3); 2 Chron. xxxv. 22, in all of which the verb employed is the same as that in the last three examples cited above, p. 42, n. 1.   [2] 2 Chron. xx. 3: cf. now also R.S.V.

[3] 2 Chron. xxxii. 2: cf. now R.S.V. ('intended'). A similar implication of purpose, intention, or will is discernible in the use of the cognate Ugaritic term *pn*. Cf. (with caution in respect of some of the proposed examples in Hebrew) J. H. Patton, *Canaanite Parallels in the Book of Psalms* (1944), pp. 24 f. The same is also true of the Accadian term PĀNU, e.g. J. A. Knudtzon, *Die El-Amarna-Tafeln* (1915), and S. A. B. Mercer, *The Tell el-Amarna Tablets* (1939), Nos. 16, 32; 250, 57; and 295, rev. 9–10. Cf. Dhorme, op. cit., p. 47; Patton, loc. cit.

[4] 2 Kings xiv. 8, 11 (= 2 Chron. xxv. 17, 21). Cf. (of God) Gen. xxxii. 31 (EVV. 30) (J); Exod. xxxiii. 11 (E); Deut. v. 4, xxxiv. 10; Judges vi. 22; Ezek. xx. 35.

[5] See in general Gen. xxxii. 21 (EVV. 20), xxxiii. 10, xliii. 3, 5, xliv. 23, 26, xlvi. 30 (all J), xlviii. 11 (E); Exod. x. 28 f. (J); 2 Sam. iii. 13, xiv. 24, 28, 32; 2 Kings xxv. 19; Esther i. 14; Jer. lii. 25. Cf. (of God) Gen. xxxiii. 10 (J); Job xxxiii. 26, and the consonantal text of at least Exod. xxiii. 15 (JE), xxxiv. 20 (J); Ps. xlii. 3 (EVV. 2); Isa. i. 12. Cf., too, the corresponding idiom in 1 Kings x. 24 (cf. 2 Chron. ix. 23); Prov. xxix. 26: and (of God)

Probably the best example of the full development of this use (outside those instances which refer to Yahweh Himself) is that in which Hushai encourages Absalom to lead his forces in person against his father, i.e.:[1]

My advice is that the whole of Israel be assembled to thee from Dan to Beer-sheba, like the sand that is by the sea for multitude, and that thou thyself (*lit.* thy face) shouldst go along ⌈with them⌉.

This, of course, is an example of the use of פָּנִים with a suffix as a simple periphrasis for the personal pronoun; and it corresponds to the way in which the psalmist may refer to 'the salvation of my face' (EVV. 'the health of my countenance'), which is really no more than an emphatic way of saying 'my salvation'.[2] Finally a typical example of the use of this term with a reflexive force may be found in Ezekiel's description of the fate of the apostate inhabitants of Palestine as being such that they should feel a loathing 'against their own selves (בִּפְנֵיהֶם)'.[3]

2 Sam. xxi. 1; 2 Chron. vii. 14; Pss. xxiv. 6, xxvii. 8, cv. 4 (= 1 Chron. xvi. 11); Hos. v. 15. Note also the following passages, which in virtue of their reference to God are obviously not to be taken too literally, Pss. xvii. 13, 15, lxxxix. 15 (EVV. 14), xcv. 2.

[1] 2 Sam. xvii. 11, following LXX, S, V, and T, *ad fin.* (i.e. reading 'in their midst' for 'into battle' (M.T.)): EVV. (cf. now R.S.V.) 'and that thou go to battle in thine own person'. See further Deut. vii. 10; Job xl. 13; Prov. vii. 15: also the more general examples of synecdoche in Prov. xxvii. 17; Isa. iii. 15. Cf. Dhorme, op. cit., p. 59: 'Le grec πρόσωπον marque les trois degrés: le visage, le masque, la personne. Le latin *persona* en marque deux: le masque, la personne. L'hébreu passera directement du visage à la personne, dans les expressions "mon visage", "ton visage" ou "son visage" pour signifier "moi, toi, lui en personne".'

[2] i.e. in the refrain of Pss. xlii. 12 (EVV. 11) and xliii. 5; also (with a corresponding division of the consonantal text) xlii. 6 (EVV. 5). Cf. A. F. Kirkpatrick, C.B. (1902), on Ps. xliv. 16 (EVV. 15), but note that in this case the Hebrew is ambiguous, as the term under discussion may be taken here as an instance of the *second* accusative of the part most closely affected by the action (G.K., § 117*ll*): vide H. Gunkel, H.K. (1926), *in loc.*

[3] vi. 9: cf. xx. 43, xxxvi. 31; Hos. v. 5, vii. 10. It should be observed, however, that the most important examples of the foregoing use of the term פָּנִים are to be found in association with the person of Yahweh; and these are so striking as to merit attention, despite the fact that a detailed examination of the Israelite conception of God falls outside the scope of the present study (cf. p. 23, n. 1, *ad fin.*). See therefore Exod. xxxiii. 14 (J), 'I Myself will go along'; Exod. xxxiii. 15 (J), 'If Thou Thyself go not along'; Deut. iv. 37, 'And He brought thee out of Egypt in His own Person, with His own

It is wholly in line with the foregoing that the psychical functions of the *ego* (אֲנִי or אָנֹכִי) should be seen at work in the activities of such peripheral and, in particular, facial organs as the mouth, with its palate, tongue, and lips, or the eyes, and even the forehead, nose, and ears; and (as already indicated) attention should be paid to the way in which these may be referred to by synecdoche as themselves engaged in some form of personal behaviour and therefore as subject in some cases to a moral judgement.[1] Thus it is said of the mouth (פֶּה), not merely that it speaks in and of itself,[2] but that in a given case it may speak wisely or foolishly,[3] and offer praise or blame;[4] and, what is more, it is

great power'; Isa. lxiii. 9, 'His personal messenger [EVV., R.S.V. the angel of his presence] saved them', or better (following LXX), 'No envoy or messenger, but He Himself saved them'; Lam. iv. 16, 'Yahweh Himself hath scattered them'. The foregoing instances are clear enough, but the following passages may be added as offering two more possible, even probable, examples: Exod. xx. 3 (E) = Deut. v. 7, 'Thou shalt have no other god beside Myself'; Ps. xxi. 10 (EVV. 9), 'Make them as a furnace of fire / In Thine own good time, Yahweh'. In the former case, cf. W. F. Albright, *From the Stone Age to Christianity*, 2nd edit. (1946), pp. 227, 331 f., 367, 2nd edit. with a New Introduction (1957), p. 297; and the fuller discussion by J. J. Stamm, *Der Dekalog im Lichte der neueren Forschung* (1958), pp. 31 ff., *Le Décalogue à la lumière des recherches contemporaines*, C.T. 43 (1959), pp. 38 f., and in *T.R.* xxvii (1961), pp. 237 ff. In the second case the insertion of the adjective 'good' in the writer's rendering, besides reproducing the force of the Hebrew in accordance with a common English idiom, also serves to reproduce the rhythm of the original; otherwise the expression in question may be rendered equally well by saying simply 'in Thine own time'. For the resultant implication of purpose or will, see above, p. 43, n. 3. Other examples *may* occur in Pss. xi. 7, xxxi. 21 (EVV. 20). All in all, therefore, the so-called 'shewbread' (לֶחֶם הַפָּנִים) appears to have been what we should call Yahweh's 'personal' bread, just as the table upon which it was placed was His 'personal' table. Cf. Exod. xxv. 30 (P); 1 Sam. xxi. 7, &c.; and Num. iv. 7 (P). (Bear in mind, too, the Punic פן בעל, like the Phoenician שם בעל, as in G. A. Cooke, *A Text-book of North-Semitic Inscriptions* (1903), pp. 131 ff.)

[1] On the question of synecdoche, note the elevated language of Pss. xvii. 10 and lxvi. 17, i.e. of the type referred to below, p. 64, n. 1.

[2] Gen. xlv. 12 (E); Pss. lxvi. 14, cxlv. 21: cf. Ps. lxxi. 15; Prov. xviii. 6. Cf., too, (of God) Isa. i. 20, xl. 5, lviii. 14; Jer. ix. 11 (EVV. 12); Mic. iv. 4; also Isa. xxxiv. 16, lxii. 2.

[3] (*a*) Pss. xxxvii. 30, xlix. 4 (EVV. 3): cf. Prov. x. 31, xvi. 23: (*b*) Isa. ix. 16: cf. Prov. xv. 2, 14 (Q), 28; also Ps. cxliv. 8, 11.

[4] (*a*) Ps. lxiii. 6 (EVV. 5); Prov. xxvii. 2: (*b*) Job ix. 20, xv. 6. Cf. 2 Sam. i. 16.

also associated in a corresponding way with ethical terms, being linked for the most part with crookedness and falsity.[1] Much the same holds good occasionally of the palate (חֵךְ), which is said in certain cases not only to taste[2] but also as an organ of speech to pronounce moral judgements,[3] speak the truth,[4] or commit sin.[5] Similarly the tongue (לָשׁוֹן) is said, not merely to speak[6] or sing,[7] but also to plan[8] or be contentious;[9] and accordingly in certain circumstances it may be referred to on the one hand as speaking constructively, e.g. with justice and knowledge,[10] or on the other hand as being responsible for boastfulness,[11] slander,[12] deceit,[13] and the like.[14] The lips again (שְׂפָתַיִם), besides being referred to as speaking[15] or exulting[16] or even as betraying fear by their quivering,[17] are said in various contexts to preserve knowledge,[18] bestow praise,[19] or be involved in dispute;[20] and they too may be described in ethical terms as capable of truthfulness[21] or charm,[22] and as being correspondingly

---

[1] Cf. in general Pss. lv. 22 (EVV. 21), cix. 2; Prov. iv. 24, vi. 12, viii. 13, x. 32, xxvi. 28; also Pss. xvii. 3, lix. 13 (EVV. 12); Prov. xvi. 10; Eccles. v. 5 (EVV. 6).

[2] Job xii. 11, xxxiv. 3.   [3] Job vi. 30: cf. Ps. cxix. 103.
[4] Prov. viii. 7.   [5] Job xxxi. 30: cf. Prov. v. 3.

[6] Job xxvii. 4, xxxiii. 2; Pss. xii. 4 (EVV. 3), xxxv. 28, xxxvii. 30, lxxi. 24; Isa. xxxii. 4, lix. 3; Jer. ix. 4, 7 (EVV. 5, 8): cf. Isa. iii. 8, xlv. 23.

[7] Ps. cxix. 172: cf. Ps. li. 16 (EVV. 14); Isa. xxxv. 6.
[8] Ps. lii. 4 (EVV. 2): cf. Ps. l. 19.   [9] Isa. liv. 17.
[10] Ps. xxxvii. 30; Prov. xv. 2, 4.
[11] Ps. xii. 4 (EVV. 3): cf. Ps. lxxiii. 9; Hos. vii. 16 (?).

[12] Ps. cxl. 12 (EVV. 11); Prov. xxv. 23. Cf., for example, G. A. Cooke, I.C.C. (1936), on Ezek. xxxvi. 3.

[13] Job xxvii. 4; Pss. l. 19, lii. 4, 6 (EVV. 2, 4), cix. 2, cxx. 2, 3; Prov. vi. 17, 24, x. 31, xii. 19, xxi. 6, xxvi. 28; Jer. ix. 4, 7 (EVV. 5, 8); Mic. vi. 12; Zeph. iii. 13.

[14] Prov. xvii. 4; Isa. lix. 3.

[15] Job xxvii. 4, xxxiii. 3; Ps. xxxiv. 14 (EVV. 13); Prov. xxiii. 16, xxiv. 2; Isa. lix. 3.

[16] Ps. lxxi. 23: cf. Job viii. 21; Ps. lxiii. 6 (EVV. 5).
[17] Hab. iii. 16.

[18] Prov. v. 2; Mal. ii. 7: cf. Prov. x. 13, 32, xiv. 7, xv. 7, xvi. 10, 21, 23, xx. 15, xxii. 17 f.

[19] Pss. lxiii. 4 (EVV. 3), cxix. 171; Prov. xxvii. 2.
[20] Job xiii. 6, xv. 6; Prov. xviii. 6: cf. (of God) Isa. xxx. 27.
[21] Job xxxiii. 3; Prov. viii. 7, xii. 19, xvi. 13, xvii. 7a, xxiii. 16.
[22] Prov. xvi. 21, xxii. 11.

helpful,[1] or again as the instruments of deceitfulness[2] and indeed mischief in general.[3]

What is true of the mouth, with its palate, tongue, and lips, is equally true of the eye (עַיִן), which is frequently referred to as itself seeing whatever may be the particular object of vision; and, what is more, it may be said not merely to see or to watch,[4] but to watch carefully.[5] Indeed to refer to the eye or the eyes as turned towards or fixed upon an object is a frequent method of indicating the concentration of one's attention,[6] just as wandering eyes betray inattention and, therefore, may be regarded by a teacher as the mark of a fool.[7] In this way the eye is regarded as instrumental in arriving at a judgement or decision in any given circumstances; so that it becomes equally idiomatic to say that a particular person or action may find favour or be good or evil 'in one's eyes', and so on.[8] Indeed the behaviour of the

---

[1] Prov. x. 21: cf. xiv. 3.

[2] Pss. xii. 3, 4 (EVV. 2, 3), xvii. 1, xxxi. 19 (EVV. 18), xxxiv. 14 (EVV. 13), cxx. 2; Prov. iv. 24, vii. 21, x. 18, xii. 22, xvii. 7b, xxvi. 23; Isa. lix. 3.

[3] Job xxvii. 4; Ps. cxl. 10 (EVV. 9); Prov. xii. 13, xvii. 4, xxiv. 2; Mal. ii. 6.

[4] The following are a few representative examples of the most common type, i.e. in association with the verb רָאָה: Gen. xlv. 12 (E); Deut. iv. 9, x. 21; 1 Sam. xxiv. 11 (EVV. 10); 2 Sam. xxiv. 3; 1 Kings x. 7; 2 Kings xxii. 20; Job xxviii. 10, xlii. 5; Pss. xxxv. 21, liv. 9 (EVV. 7); Prov. xxiii. 33; Isa. vi. 5, xxxiii. 20; Jer. xxxiv. 3; Mic. vii. 10; Mal. i. 5. Cf. the following selected examples of a rarer type, i.e. in association with a different verb: (a) Isa. xxxiii. 7; Mic. iv. 11: cf. (of God) Pss. xi. 4, xvii. 2: (b) Ps. xcii. 12 (EVV. 11); Prov. iv. 25: cf. (of the vulture) Job xxxix. 29: (c) Job vii. 8, xxiv. 15b: (d) Job xx. 9: cf. (of the falcon) xxviii. 7.

[5] Job xxiv. 15a; Prov. xxiii. 26 (Q): cf. Ps. x. 8; and (of God) Ps. lxvi. 7; Prov. xv. 3. Cf., too, (of the eyelids) Prov. iv. 25.

[6] Cf. (a) Num. xi. 6 (J); Pss. xxv. 15, cxxiii. 2, cxli. 8: cf. (of God) Pss. xxxiii. 18, xxxiv. 16 (EVV. 15): (b) 1 Kings i. 20; 2 Chron. xx. 12; Jer. xxii. 17: cf. (of God) Ps. xxxii. 8: (c) Ruth ii. 9; Ps. ci. 6: cf. (of God) Deut. xi. 12; Prov. xv. 3; Amos ix. 8. Cf., too, such idioms of a verbal type as (a) Gen. xxxix. 7 (J); Deut. iii. 27; Pss. cxxi. 1, cxxiii. 1; Isa. li. 6; Ezek. xviii. 6, 15, xxiii. 27, xxxiii. 25: (b) Ps. xvii. 11; Jer. xxiv. 6 (of God), xl. 4; Amos ix. 4 (of God): (c) 1 Kings viii. 29, 52 (cf. 2 Chron. vi. 20, 40); 2 Chron. vii. 15; Neh. i. 6; Job xiv. 3; Jer. xxxii. 19; Zech. xii. 4 (all of God): and see also (d) 2 Chron. xvi. 9 (of God); Ps. cxlv. 15. [7] Prov. xvii. 24.

[8] e.g. (a) Gen. xxxiii. 8 (J); Ruth ii. 10; 1 Sam. xvi. 22: (b) Gen. xli. 37 (E); 1 Sam. xxix. 6; 1 Kings xxi. 2: (c) Gen. xxi. 11 (E); 1 Sam. viii. 6: and so often. Cf. Job xxix. 11, as quoted below in the text; also, with reference to the eyelids, Ps. xi. 4 (of God).

eye is found to be related to a wide range of psychical activity, i.e. pride or humility,[1] favour or disfavour,[2] desire and hope,[3] or disappointment;[4] and in view of the ease with which the eye may be affected by distress of any kind[5] it is not surprising that it should be found capable of pity.[6] Nor is it surprising, all in all, that the eyes should be subject to a moral judgement, so that one may think in terms of a good or an evil eye.[7] In fact the eyes are found to be so expressive (readily betraying any fluctuation in a man's vigour or alertness)[8] that occasionally the use of the term is almost equivalent to that of נֶפֶשׁ or פָּנִים, when these are employed with reference to the individual as a whole. One of the most striking examples is that afforded by the author of the book of Job, when he includes the adulterer amongst the enemies of the light by saying:[9]

And the eye of the adulterer waiteth for the twilight,

---

[1] (a) Pss. xviii. 28 (EVV. 27), cxxxi. 1; Prov. vi. 17, xxx. 13; Isa. ii. 11, x. 12: cf. Ps. ci. 5; Prov. xxi. 4; Isa. v. 15; also 2 Kings xix. 22 (= Isa. xxxvii. 23); Prov. xxx. 17: (b) Job xxii. 29. Cf. (of the eyelids) Prov. xxx. 13.

[2] Cf. p. 47, n. 8, and such passages as (a) Ps. ci. 6; Jer. xl. 4: also (of God) Deut. xi. 12; Pss. xxxii. 8, xxxiii. 18, xxxiv. 16 (EVV. 15); Jer. xxiv. 6: (b) Amos ix. 4, 8 (of God).

[3] Cf., for example, (a) Gen. iii. 6 (J); Num. xv. 39 (P); 1 Kings xx. 6; Job xxxi. 1; Eccles. ii. 10 (cf. i. 8, iv. 8); Jer. xxii. 17; Lam. ii. 4; Ezek. xxiv. 16, 21, 25; and the idiom of the type represented by Pss. xxxv. 21, liv. 9 (EVV. 7), xcii. 12 (EVV. 11); Mic. iv. 11, vii. 10: (b) 2 Chron. xx. 12; Pss. xxv. 15, cxxi. 1, cxxiii. 1, 2, cxli. 8, cxlv. 15. Cf., too, 1 Kings i. 20.

[4] e.g. Job xi. 20, xxxi. 16; Pss. lxix. 4 (EVV. 3), cxix. 82; Lam. iv. 17.

[5] e.g. Deut. xxviii. 65; 1 Sam. ii. 33; Job xi. 20, xvii. 7, xxxi. 16; Pss. vi. 8 (EVV. 7), xxxi. 10 (EVV. 9), lxix. 4 (EVV. 3), lxxxviii. 10 (EVV. 9), cxix. 82, 123, 136; Jer. viii. 23 (EVV. ix. 1), ix. 17 (EVV. 18), xiv. 17, xxxi. 16; Lam. i. 16, ii. 11, 18, iii. 48, 49 (cf. 51), iv. 17, v. 17.

[6] Gen. xlv. 20 (E); Deut. vii. 16, xiii. 9 (EVV. 8), xix. 13, 21, xxv. 12; Isa. xiii. 18; Ezek. ix. 5, xvi. 5: cf. (of God) Ezek. v. 11, vii. 4, 9, viii. 18, ix. 10, xx. 17.

[7] (a) cf. Prov. xxii. 9: (b) Deut. xv. 9, xxviii. 54, 56: cf. Prov. xxiii. 6, xxviii. 22. Cf. (a) Hab. i. 13 (of God): (b) Job xv. 12, xvi. 9; Prov. vi. 13, xvi. 30.

[8] Cf. 1 Sam. xiv. 27 (Q), 29; Ezra ix. 8; Pss. xiii. 4 (EVV. 3), xix. 9 (EVV. 8); Prov. xxix. 13.

[9] Job xxiv. 15: cf. Ps. cxix. 82, 148; Prov. xxx. 17; Jer. xxxii. 4, xxxiv. 3: also (of God) Prov. xxii. 12; Isa. iii. 8. Cf. the secondary use of the term עַיִן to denote the 'surface' or 'appearance' of an object: (a) Exod. x. 5, 15 (J); Num. xxii. 5, 11 (JE): (b) Lev. xiii. 55; Num. xi. 7 (JE), &c.

Saying, 'No eye shall see me';
And he putteth on a covering for the face.

The forcefulness of the idiom makes the author's language extraordinarily picturesque, but, of course, it is merely another example of the common linguistic device known as synecdoche; i.e., as the context shows, such a use of the term under discussion should not be taken literally as pointing to anything like a supposed 'diffusion of consciousness' in the Israelite conception of man, and the same must be said when one finds the eye referred to as 'showing pity' or the like (as above).[1]

Again, as is well known, the fact that the nostrils are used primarily for breathing,[2] and that one's normal cool breathing is unmistakably quickened with the kindling and mounting of one's wrath,[3] has meant that the term אַף, besides being used of the 'nostril', and so by synecdoche of the 'nose' and (in the dual אַפַּיִם) of the 'face', is also used by metonymy to denote 'anger';[4] and, of course, to have one's

[1] Cf. p. 48, n. 6: and for the theory of a 'diffusion of consciousness', see below, p. 81, n. 5.

[2] Cf. Gen. ii. 7 (J), vii. 22 (J); Job xxvii. 3; Isa. ii. 22; Lam. iv. 20: also (of God) Exod. xv. 8 (J); 2 Sam. xxii. 16 (cf. Ps. xviii. 16 (EVV. 15)); and probably (in view of the parallelism) Job iv. 9.

[3] The short, sharp breathing observable in the action of one's nostrils apparently suggested one of the idioms for impatience, just as the corresponding idiom for patience appears to be based upon the observation of man's normal, deep breathing. Cf. the Hebrew of (a) Prov. xiv. 17: (b) Prov. xiv. 29, xv. 18, xvi. 32, xix. 11, xxv. 15: also (of God) Exod. xxxiv. 6 (J), &c.; Isa. xlviii. 9; Jer. xv. 15. Accordingly it is conceivable that the similar idioms associated with the terms נֶפֶשׁ and רוּחַ should be thought of in the same way. See above, p. 12, nn. 7 and 8, and p. 30, n. 12: and in the case of רוּחַ, cf. Dhorme, op. cit., p. 81. For the kindling of one's wrath, note the common use of אַף with the verb חָרָה ('to burn'); and for an excellent example of the effect which mounting wrath was observed to have upon the nostrils, see the striking anthropomorphism in Ezek. xxxviii. 18 (which, significantly enough, has been eliminated in LXX).

[4] For the meaning 'face', cf. Accadian APPU (dual APPĀ) and especially, of course, Aramaic including Syriac, e.g. ܐܦܶ̈ܐ. The uniformity of the meanings 'nose' and 'face' (as opposed to 'anger') in the cognate languages makes it probable, if not certain, that in this case the purely physical meaning is the earlier, and one may compare the example of metonymy furnished by the use of the term 'tongue', in Hebrew as elsewhere, to denote 'speech' or 'language'. Cf. in general König, *Stilistik, Rhetorik, Poetik, &c.*, pp. 17 ff.

nose in the air, as we say, was for the Israelite as for us an obvious sign of pride.[1]

Similarly the set of the forehead (מֵצַח) may betray determination (not to say obstinacy)[2] and even impudence,[3] while the ear (אֹזֶן) not only fulfils its proper function of hearing,[4] but in doing so may be described in certain circumstances as attentive,[5] or seeking knowledge,[6] or showing understanding and discrimination.[7] In such a case, however, one must again beware of taking too literally what is obviously poetical language and construing this in terms of a supposed 'diffusion of consciousness', as has been done, for example, in the case of Job xxix. 11:[8]

> When the ear heard, it pronounced me happy;
> And when the eye saw, it bore witness to me.

This no more points to a 'diffusion of consciousness' than does Proverbs xv. 31:

> The ear that hearkeneth to vital instruction
> Will dwell among the wise.

What we have in each case is that form of synecdoche to which attention has already been drawn, whereby in certain circumstances an important part of one's נֶפֶשׁ or person acquires a heightened significance, and so may be used picturesquely and graphically with reference to the individual as a whole.

Of the peripheral parts of the body other than those associated with the head it is in the arm (אֶזְרוֹעַ/זְרוֹעַ) and especially the hand (יָד) with its palm (כַּף) and fingers (sing. אֶצְבַּע) that the Israelite conception of man as a

---

[1] Ps. x. 4: cf. the German 'Hochnäsigkeit'.
[2] Isa. xlviii. 4; Ezek. iii. 7–9.　　　　　　　　　　　　　[3] Jer. iii. 3.
[4] e.g. 2 Sam. xxii. 45 (cf. Ps. xviii. 45 (EVV. 44)); Job xiii. 1, xlii. 5; Ps. xcii. 12 (EVV. 11); Prov. xv. 31, xx. 12, xxv. 12; Eccles. i. 8; Isa. xxx. 21, l. 4: cf. Job iv. 12; Jer. ix. 19 (EVV. 20); also (by contrast) Mic. vii. 16.
[5] Isa. xxxii. 3: also (of God) 2 Chron. vi. 40, vii. 15; Neh. i. 6, 11; Ps. cxxx. 2. Cf. Neh. viii. 3: and see below, p. 81, n. 5.
[6] Prov. xviii. 15.　　　　　　[7] (a) Job xiii. 1: (b) Job xii. 11, xxxiv. 3.
[8] Cf. H. W. Robinson, *Inspiration and Revelation in the Old Testament*, p. 72: and see below, p. 81, n. 5.

psycho-physical organism and as a centre of power manifests itself most clearly. Thus the arm, as in the picturesque reference to its being bared for action,[1] is commonly associated with the thought of strength, whether this be for an aggressive or for a defensive purpose;[2] and as a result it sometimes occurs with a certain emphasis upon the power to lend support.[3] What is more, in thus providing a ready measure of one's vitality it is equally readily used by synecdoche for one's person as a whole. A particularly good example is that which is afforded by Job's ironical words to Bildad:[4]

> How hast thou helped *him that is powerless*,
> Hast thou saved *the strengthless arm*!

—or by Isaiah's description of the impending doom of Ephraim:[5]

> It shall be as when *the reaper gathereth* the corn,
> When *his arm doth reap* the ears.

[1] Ezek. iv. 7: cf. (of God) Isa. lii. 10; also liii. 1.

[2] 1 Sam. ii. 31; Job xxii. 8, 9, xxxv. 9; Pss. x. 15, xxxvii. 17; Prov. xxxi. 17; Isa. xliv. 12; Jer. xlviii. 25; Ezek. xvii. 9, xxii. 6, xxx. 21, 22, 24, 25; Dan. xi. 6; Hos. vii. 15: and (of God) Exod. xv. 16 (J); Job xl. 9; Pss. lxxi. 18, lxxvii. 15 f. (EVV. 14 f.), lxxix. 11, lxxxix. 11, 14 (EVV. 10, 13); Isa. xlviii. 14, li. 9, liii. 1, lxii. 8. Note especially the association of such power with Yahweh's 'outstretched Arm' which is so characteristic of D, particularly in the recurrent reference to His 'strong Hand and outstretched Arm', i.e. Deut. iv. 34, v. 15, vii. 19, xi. 2, xxvi. 8; 1 Kings viii. 42; 2 Chron. vi. 32; Ps. cxxxvi. 12; Jer. xxxii. 21; Ezek. xx. 33, 34: cf. Exod. vi. 6 (P); Deut. ix. 29; 2 Kings xvii. 36; Jer. xxi. 5, xxvii. 5, xxxii. 17, 21. Note too that in Dan. xi. 15, 22, and 31 the plural is used with obvious reference to military 'forces': and on this point see Dhorme, op. cit., p. 141.

[3] 2 Chron. xxxii. 8; Ps. lxxxiii. 9 (EVV. 8); Jer. xvii. 5; Ezek. xxxi. 17: and (of God) Deut. xxxiii. 27; Isa. xxxiii. 2.   [4] xxvi. 2.

[5] xvii. 5 (cf. R.V., R.S.V.). It is conceivable, of course, that in this instance we have an example of the construction referred to below, p. 64, n. 1 (cf. A.V.); and this is perhaps the more likely in that the noun under discussion is commonly construed as feminine. This is not always so, however (cf., for example, Isa. li. 5); and in either case the argument in the text holds good. See further Gen. xlix. 24 (J): also (of both man and God) Ps. xliv. 4 (EVV. 3); and (of God) Pss. lxxxix. 22 (EVV. 21), xcviii. 1; Isa. xl. 10, li. 5, 9 f., lix. 16, lxiii. 5, 12. Of the foregoing passages Isa. li. 9 f., with its vivid 'personification' of the Arm of Yahweh, is particularly instructive. There is some doubt in the case of 2 Sam. xxii. 35 (= Ps. xviii. 35 (EVV. 34)), while the text of Dan. xi. 6 provides an interesting example of ambiguity: vide comm., *in loc.*

The parallelism in both these passages makes the presence of synecdoche perfectly clear, and reveals that there is nothing here which may be said to spring from any belief in a 'diffusion of consciousness'. For the rest, what is said of the arm is said more frequently and more strikingly of the hand, which was obviously found to be of quite extraordinary importance as a measure of one's vitality and as a revelation of one's mood, purpose, or character.[1]

Of the two hands the right is usually the more active[2] and the more significant;[3] and to be left-handed is to be the subject of special comment.[4] Accordingly to be at someone's right hand is to be in the place of honour,[5] and to have someone at one's right hand is normally to enjoy his protection or support.[6] In general, however, we may note first that, as is to be expected, the many and varied activities of the hands provided a ready index to one's feelings, and so might betoken a wide range of mood involving grief and shame,[7] simple supplication (especially in the raising or

---

[1] Cf. (in addition to the works of H. W. Robinson and especially that of Dhorme, which are cited above, p. 4, n. 1) L. H. Brockington, 'The Hand of Man and the Hand of God', *B.Q.* x (1940), pp. 191–7; also (with caution) M. A. Canney, *Givers of Life* (1923), pp. 88–103. Note, too, that the term כַּף, which properly denotes the hollow or palm of the hand, is often used by synecdoche for the hand itself, as will be clear from some of the passages cited in the following notes. Cf., for example, Gen. xxxi. 42 (E); Deut. xxv. 12; Pss. ix. 17 (EVV. 16), lxxviii. 72; Prov. x. 4, xxxi. 13, 16: and so often.

[2] Cf. Judges v. 26; Job xl. 14; Pss. xxi. 9 (EVV. 8), xlv. 5 (EVV. 4), lxxxix. 26, 43 (EVV. 25, 42), cxxxvii. 5; Isa. lxiii. 12; Ezek. xxi. 27 (EVV. 22): also (of God) Exod. xv. 6, 12 (both J); Pss. xvii. 7, xviii. 36 (EVV. 35), xx. 7 (EVV. 6), xliv. 4 (EVV. 3), lx. 7 (EVV. 5) = cviii. 7 (EVV. 6), lxiii. 9 (EVV. 8), lxxiv. 11, lxxvii. 11 (EVV. 10), lxxviii. 54, lxxxix. 14 (EVV. 13), xcviii. 1, cxviii. 15 f., cxxxviii. 7, cxxxix. 10; Isa. xlviii. 13; Lam. ii. 3 f.

[3] Cf. Gen. xlviii. 8–22 (JE), as cited below, p. 58, n. 6; Eccles. x. 2: also (of God) Jer. xxii. 24.

[4] Judges iii. 15, xx. 16: cf. 1 Chron. xii. 2 (all with reference to members of the tribe of Benjamin as left-handed or ambidextrous).

[5] Cf. 1 Kings ii. 19; Ps. xlv. 10 (EVV. 9): also (of God) Pss. lxxx. 18 (EVV. 17), cx. 1.

[6] Cf. Pss. xvi. 8, lxxiii. 23, cix. 31, cx. 5, cxxi. 5, cxlii. 5 (EVV. 4); Isa. xli. 13, xlv. 1; also, perhaps, Ps. xci. 7: but note that in the law-courts, apparently, it was customary for the accuser to stand at the right hand of the defendant, Ps. cix. 6; Zech. iii. 1.

[7] 2 Sam. xiii. 19; Jer. ii. 37 (cf. xxx. 6).

spreading of the hands in the formal act of prayer),[1] or again (in the waving and clapping of the hands) both repugnance[2] and exultation.[3]

In the nature of the case, however, their employment for all sorts of practical ends made them appear not only expressive but peculiarly powerful; and this association of the hand with the thought of power is so primitive as well as persistent that it comes to the fore in a number of common idioms, although in such cases (as in some others which we shall have occasion to note) the literal meaning must not be pressed, inasmuch as the language is obviously formal and often purely figurative or metaphorical.[4] Thus when stress was being laid upon one's ability to perform a particular action, one might speak, not merely of '*my* power' and the like, but also of 'the power *of my hand*'. In the book of Deuteronomy, for example, the Israelites are warned against thinking that the prosperity attendant upon the conquest of Canaan was due to their own ability, in fact against being tempted to say to themselves:[5]

[1] (*a*) Prov. i. 24; Lam. i. 17: similarly (of God) Isa. lxv. 2 (cf. xxv. 11?): (*b*) see Neh. viii. 6; Pss. xxviii. 2, lxxvii. 3 (EVV. 2) (?), cxxxiv. 2, cxliii. 6: and especially (with literal reference to the palm) Exod. ix. 29, 33 (both J); 1 Kings viii. 22, 38, 54 (cf. 2 Chron. vi. 12, 29); 2 Chron. vi. 13; Ezra ix. 5; Job xi. 13; Pss. xliv. 21 (EVV. 20), lxiii. 5 (EVV. 4), lxxxviii. 10 (EVV. 9), cxix. 48, cxli. 2; Isa. i. 15; Jer. iv. 31; Lam. ii. 19, iii. 41. Cf. perhaps Pss. lxviii. 32 (EVV. 31), lxxvii. 3 (EVV. 2): also the use of the hand in throwing a kiss to the sun or the moon, Job xxxi. 27.

[2] (*a*) Zeph. ii. 15: (*b*) Num. xxiv. 10 (J); Job xxvii. 23; Lam. ii. 15: cf. (of God) Ezek. xxii. 13.

[3] Ezek. xxv. 6. Cf. (again with literal reference to the palm) 2 Kings xi. 12; Ps. xlvii. 2 (EVV. 1); Ezek. vi. 11, xxi. 19 (EVV. 14); Nahum iii. 19: also Ps. xcviii. 8; Isa. lv. 12; and (of God) Ezek. xxi. 22 (EVV. 17).

[4] Cf. the following note, *ad fin.*

[5] Deut. viii. 17: cf. (of God) Job xxx. 21. Cf. (*a*) Job xxx. 2; Isa. x. 13: (*b*) (of God) Exod. xiii. 3, 14, 16 (all J); Isa. viii. 11. Probably the idiom represented by יֶשׁ־לְאֵל יָדִי and its parallels should also be included here: e.g. Gen. xxxi. 29 (E), where Laban is reported as saying to Jacob, 'It is in the power of my hand to do you hurt' (EVV.). Cf. Deut. xxviii. 32; Neh. v. 5; Prov. iii. 27; Mic. ii. 1. It has been suggested, of course, that this expression should be traced back to a belief in spirits as animating or influencing various organs of the body. Cf. C. Brockelmann, *Z.A.W.* xxvi (1906), pp. 29 ff.; and note that this suggestion is followed by H. W. Robinson in his attempt to establish the theory of a 'diffused consciousness' in the Hebrew conception

It is *my power* and *the might of my hand* that hath gained me this wealth.

Similarly to do a thing 'with a strong hand' is to demonstrate one's power, as when it is said that during the period of the wandering in the desert Edom came out 'with much people and with a strong hand' against Israel.[1] Indeed the term for 'hand' (יָד) is occasionally used as a simple synonym for 'power'.[2]

What is more, the action of the hand also affords an indication of one's purpose as well as one's power; for, far from being thought of as operating independently,[3] it appears to be recognized from the first as controlled by its owner, who is said to 'send' it out when he extends it for

of man. Cf. *Inspiration and Revelation in the Old Testament*, p. 73: and see below, p. 81, n. 5. However, even if Brockelmann's suggestion be sound (and in the present writer's opinion this is extremely doubtful), the expression in question is too idiomatic to be regarded as other than a survival from a more primitive period; it may hardly be treated as valid evidence for the currency of the belief at a later date.

[1] Num. xx. 20 (JE). Cf. Judges iii. 10, vi. 2: and (of God) Ps. lxxxix. 14 (EVV. 13). This, of course, is a familiar way of referring to Yahweh's intervention on behalf of His people, notably in the deliverance from Egypt, which He is said to have effected 'with great power and with a strong Hand'. Exod. xxxii. 11 (JE). Cf. (as cited in part above, p. 51, n. 2) Exod. iii. 19 (E), vi. 1 (J), xiii. 9 (J); Deut. iii. 24, iv. 34, v. 15, vi. 21, vii. 8, 19, ix. 26, xi. 2, xxvi. 8; 1 Kings viii. 42; 2 Chron. vi. 32; Neh. i. 10; Ps. cxxxvi. 12; Jer. xxxii. 21; Ezek. xx. 33, 34; Dan. ix. 15. Cf. too (*a*) Deut. xxxiv. 12, as cited in the following note: (*b*) Exod. xiii. 3, 14, 16 (all J), as cited in the preceding note: and (*c*) the way in which a prophet, when in a state of 'possession' or 'ecstasy', could be thought of (or could think of himself) as being firmly in the grip of God, i.e. of Yahweh's Hand as being not merely upon him (1 Kings xviii. 46; 2 Kings iii. 15; Ezek. i. 3, iii. 22, viii. 1, xxxiii. 22, xxxvii. 1, xl. 1) but even 'strong' upon him, i.e. Ezek. iii. 14: cf. Isa. viii. 11, as cited in the preceding note. See also 1 Chron. xxix. 12; 2 Chron. xx. 6; Jer. xvi. 21. Finally, note the use of the term for hand without an accompanying adjective to denote God's power or activity, i.e. in Exod. xvi. 3 (P); Job xxvii. 11; Pss. lxxviii. 42, cix. 27; Jer. xv. 17: and contrast with this its use without further definition of any kind to denote human as opposed to divine action, i.e. in Job xxxiv. 20; Dan. viii. 25.

[2] i.e. (*a*) in the singular, Exod. xiv. 31 (J); Deut. xxxii. 36, xxxiv. 12; Isa. xxviii. 2; Dan. xii. 7: (*b*) in the dual, Joshua viii. 20: cf. Ps. lxxvi. 6 (EVV. 5); Isa. xlv. 9.

[3] Cf. Brockington, op. cit., p. 192, *ad init.*; also as cited below, p. 81, n. 5.

any particular purpose, e.g. to take hold of an object,[1] help those in need,[2] make an attack upon someone,[3] or simply engage in daily toil.[4] Indeed, the same is true of the finger, which is thus referred to as being pointed in a gesture of mockery or derision;[5] and it is in this light, therefore, that we must read the words of the psalmist, when he says:[6]

> Blessed be Yahweh, my Rock,
> Who traineth my hands for battle,
> My fingers for the fight!

Accordingly, it is also idiomatic to speak of someone's hand as being laid upon one in judgement and the like,[7] or as resting upon one for defensive or offensive purposes, for good[8] or ill,[9] and in such a case as sometimes doing so heavily,[10] severely,[11] or strongly.[12] Indeed, a whole series of

---

[1] Gen. iii. 22 (J), viii. 9 (J), xix. 10 (J), xxii. 10 (J); Exod. iv. 4 (J), xxii. 7, 10 (EVV. 8, 11); Deut. xxv. 11; Judges v. 26, xv. 15; 1 Sam. xvii. 49; 2 Sam. xv. 5; 2 Kings vi. 7; 1 Chron. xiii. 9 f. (cf. 2 Sam. vi. 6); Esther ix. 10, 15, 16; Prov. xxxi. 19. Cf. Ps. cxxv. 3; Song of Sol. v. 4; Isa. xi. 14; also Ezek. x. 7. [2] Prov. xxxi. 20: cf. (of God) Jer. i. 9.

[3] Gen. xxii. 12 (E), xxxvii. 22 (E); 1 Sam. xxii. 17, xxiv. 7, 11 (EVV. 6, 10), xxvi. 9, 11, 23; 2 Sam. i. 14, xviii. 12; 1 Kings xiii. 4; Neh. xiii. 21; Esther ii. 21, iii. 6, vi. 2, viii. 7, ix. 2; Ps. lv. 21 (EVV. 20); Dan. xi. 42. Cf. Job xxviii. 9: also (of God and His heavenly ministers) Exod. iii. 20 (E), ix. 15 (J), xxiv. 11 (J); 2 Sam. xxiv. 16; Job i. 11, 12, ii. 5; Ps. cxxxviii. 7.

[4] Cf. the special significance attaching to the phrase of the type מִשְׁלַח יָדֶ֔ךָ, which is peculiar to Deuteronomy, i.e. xii. 7, 18, xv. 10, xxiii. 21 (EVV. 20), xxviii. 8, 20: also the synonymous מַעֲשֵׂה יָדֶ֔ךָ and its parallels, as referred to below, p. 60, n. 3.

[5] Isa. lviii. 9. Cf. Prov. vi. 13: also (as indicating the will of God) Exod. viii. 15 (EVV. 19) (P), xxxi. 18 (E); Deut. ix. 10.

[6] Ps. cxliv. 1: cf. 2 Sam. xxii. 35 = Ps. xviii. 35 (EVV. 34); and see below, p. 60, n. 4.

[7] Cf. 1 Chron. xviii. 3 (as against 2 Sam. viii. 3); Job ix. 33; Ps. lxxix. 26 (EVV. 25): also (of God) Exod. vii. 4 (P); Ezek. xxxix. 21; and (with literal reference to the palm) Ps. cxxxix. 5.

[8] 2 Chron. xxx. 12; Ezra vii. 6, 9, 28, viii. 18, 22, 31; Neh. ii. 8, 18; Ps. lxxx. 18 (EVV. 17): cf. 1 Chron. iv. 10; Pss. lxxxviii. 6 (EVV. 5), lxxxix. 22 (EVV. 21); Isa. xlix. 2, lxvi. 14 (all of God).

[9] Gen. xvi. 12 (J), xxxvii. 27 (J); Deut. xiii. 10 (EVV. 9), xvii. 7; 1 Sam. xviii. 17, 21, xxiv. 13, 14 (EVV. 12, 13): also (of God) Exod. ix. 3 (J); Deut. ii. 15; Judges ii. 15; Ruth i. 13; 1 Sam. v. 9, vii. 13, xii. 15; 2 Sam. xxiv. 17; 1 Chron. xxi. 17; Ps. xxxviii. 3 (EVV. 2); Ezek. xiii. 9.

[10] 1 Sam. v. 6, 11; Ps. xxxii. 4 (all of God): cf. Judges i. 35.

[11] Judges iv. 24; and (of God) 1 Sam. v. 7. [12] Judges iii. 10, vi. 2.

common prepositional phrases reveals the thought that to be 'in', 'upon', or 'under' someone's hand (or hands) is to be in his power, and therefore under his protection or subject to his direction and control; and that, correspondingly, to be delivered 'from' someone's hand is to escape from his power, and so on.[1]

Further, as one might expect, an assertive or aggressive purpose is also indicated by the raising,[2] swinging,[3] or stretching[4] out of the hand; so that to do anything 'with a high hand' is to act proudly or defiantly.[5] In the same way,

---

[1] Cf., for example, B.D.B., pp. 390 f. and 496, s.v. בְּ, עַל, תַּחַת, and מִן. The use of the expressions עַל־יַד and עַל־יְדֵי with their implication of being under someone's protection (Gen. xlii. 37 (E)): cf. (with literal reference to the palm) Ps. xci. 12) or subject to one's direction (e.g. 1 Chron. xxv. 2; Jer. v. 31) is specially interesting; for, though at first sight its development is less obvious, it really has a simple parallel in the English idiom 'to have someone (*or* something) *on* one's hands'. At the same time, as already indicated earlier in the text, we must beware of over-emphasizing the literal meaning of these obviously stereotyped forms. Cf. their completely metaphorical use in (*a*) Job viii. 4; Prov. xviii. 21: (*b*) 2 Chron. xxix. 27; Ps. lxiii. 11 (EVV. 10); Jer. xviii. 21; Ezek. xxxv. 5: (*c*) 1 Sam. xvii. 37; Job v. 20; Pss. xxii. 21 (EVV. 20), xlix. 16 (EVV. 15), lxxxix. 49 (EVV. 48); Isa. xlvii. 14; Dan. viii. 4, 7; Hos. xiii. 14. While on this subject of prepositional phrases and corresponding idioms, bear in mind our own use of the expressions 'to be at hand', 'to have handy', the latter of which has a close parallel in 1 Sam. ix. 8, נִמְצָא בְיָדִי, i.e. 'I have handy'. (Professor S. A. Cook, in a private communication.)

[2] (*a*) 2 Sam. xviii. 28, xx. 21; also (of God) Ps. x. 12; Isa. xlix. 22: (*b*) Num. xx. 11 (P); Deut. xxxii. 27; 1 Kings xi. 26, 27; Mic. v. 8 (EVV. 9); also (of God) Isa. xxvi. 11. Cf., too, Exod. xvii. 11 (E), as cited below, p. 59, n. 1: also (of the arm) Job xxxviii. 15, and (of God) Isa. xxx. 30.

[3] (*a*) Job xxxi. 21; Isa. x. 32, xiii. 2; also (of God) Isa. xi. 15, xix. 16; Zech. ii. 13 (EVV. 9): (*b*) Jer. vi. 9; Ezek. xxxviii. 12 (also perhaps 2 Sam. viii. 3, but see 1 Chron. xviii. 3); and especially (of God) Ps. lxxxi. 15 (EVV. 14); Isa. i. 25; Amos i. 8; Zech. xiii. 7: (*c*) Lam. iii. 3. Cf., too, 2 Kings v. 11, as cited below, p. 58, n. 5.

[4] i.e. for the most part (so far as man is concerned) with reference to the miraculous power concentrated in Aaron's rod (Exod. vii. 19 (P), viii. 1, 2, 13 (EVV. 5, 6, 17) (all P)), Moses' rod and hand (Exod. ix. 22 (E), x. 12 f., 21, 22 (all E), xiv. 16, 21, 26, 27 (all P); cf. xvii. 8–13 (E), as cited below, p. 59, n. 1), and Joshua's javelin (Joshua viii. 18 f., 26): but see also Job xv. 25. Cf. (of God) Exod. vii. 5 (P); Isa. v. 25, ix. 11, 16, 20 (EVV. 12, 17, 21), x. 4, xiv. 26, 27, xxiii. 11, xxxi. 3; Jer. vi. 12, xv. 6, xxi. 5, li. 25; Ezek. vi. 14, xiv. 9, 13, xvi. 27, xxv. 7, 13, 16, xxxv. 3; Zeph. i. 4, ii. 13. See also Lam. i. 10: and (of God) Ruth i. 13; Job vi. 9. Cf. now P. Humbert, ' "Étendre la main" ', *V.T.* xii (1962), pp. 383–95.

[5] Exod. xiv. 8 (P); Num. xv. 30 (P), xxxiii. 3 (P).

while the withdrawal of one's hand may point to mere lack of power,[1] it more often implies the achievement or the forsaking of one's purpose[2] or the conscious holding of one's power in check;[3] and similarly, while the drooping or dropping of the hands may indicate no more than mere physical weakness[4] or the simple abandonment of an action[5] or even a definite refusal to act,[6] it usually suggests sheer despondency or lack of resolution.[7] This, of course, corresponds in turn to the fact that to 'strengthen' a man's hands normally means to encourage him or make him resolute.[8] Finally, the action of the hand also affords a measure of one's generosity;[9] so that, as in English, to be 'open-handed' is to be generously inclined.[10]

Of special interest, however, is the way in which the hand is used to reinforce or give effect to the written or spoken word, not merely in fulfilling a promise or carrying out a threat and so on, but as a strictly formal procedure. Thus it was obviously the practice to ratify an agreement or endorse a pledge by shaking or clasping hands;[11] and this

---

[1] Gen. xxxviii. 29 (J). Cf. the suggestion of impotence in the idiomatic reference to 'shortness' of hand in 2 Kings xix. 26 (= Isa. xxxvii. 27): also (of God) Num. xi. 23 (J); Isa. l. 2, lix. 1.

[2] Joshua viii. 26; 1 Kings xiii. 4: also (of God) Lam. ii. 8; Ezek. xx. 22 (contrast Isa. xiv. 27). Cf. 1 Sam. xiv. 19.

[3] Ezek. xviii. 8, 17: also (of God) Ps. lxxiv. 11. Cf. Eccles. vii. 18, xi. 6.

[4] 2 Sam. xvii. 2 (cf. xxiii. 10): cf. Lev. xxv. 35 (H).

[5] Cf. (of Yahweh's Angel) 2 Sam. xxiv. 16; 1 Chron. xxi. 15.

[6] Joshua x. 6.

[7] 2 Sam. iv. 1; 2 Chron. xv. 7; Ezra iv. 4; Neh. vi. 9; Job iv. 3; Isa. xiii. 7, xxxv. 3; Jer. vi. 24, xxxviii. 4, xlvii. 3, l. 43; Ezek. vii. 17 (cf. 27), xxi. 12 (EVV. 7); Zeph. iii. 16. Cf., perhaps, Job xxiii. 2.

[8] Judges ix. 24; 1 Sam. xxiii. 16; Ezra vi. 22; Neh. ii. 18, vi. 9; Job iv. 3; Isa. xxxv. 3; Jer. xxiii. 14; Ezek. xiii. 22: cf. Judges vii. 11; 2 Sam. ii. 7, xvi. 21; Ezek. xxii. 14; Zech. viii. 9, 13. On the other hand, in the slightly different expressions of Ezra i. 6 and Ezek. xvi. 49 the emphasis appears to fall rather upon the provision of material support. Cf. the 'enlivening' of the hand in Isa. lvii. 10, as referred to below, p. 103, n. 4.

[9] 1 Kings x. 13; Esther i. 7, ii. 18. Cf. (of God's right hand) Ps. xvi. 11; also (of the right and the left hand of Wisdom) Prov. iii. 16.

[10] Deut. xv. 8, 11: cf. (of God) Pss. civ. 28, cxlv. 16. Bear in mind also the suggestion made by G. R. Driver, in *J.T.S.* xliii (1942), pp. 157 f., and xliv (1943), p. 20, apropos Ps. lx. 7 (EVV. 5), &c.

[11] Job xvii. 3; also (with literal reference to the palm) Prov. vi. 1, xvii. 18,

has a close parallel in the use of the hand to confirm an oath, i.e. either by raising the hand aloft (originally, no doubt, as a means of attracting God's attention and so ensuring an act of judgement on His part if the oath should be violated)[1] or by placing one's hand under the other man's thigh (an intimate gesture expressive of what was indeed meant to be a vital bond).[2]

Even more important in this connexion is the use of the hand in the effort to make one's power felt in magical or religio-magical fashion as a blessing or curse, whether this was expressed in actual words or was merely implicit in what one did. Such power was thought to be communicated either by touch (as in the laying of one's hand upon the head of the recipient while pronouncing an individual blessing)[3] or by a simple gesture of an appropriate kind (as in the public pronouncement of the priestly blessing[4] or the healing action which Naaman the Syrian expected of Elisha).[5] Moreover, as we learn from Israel's blessing of Ephraim and Manasseh, the right hand was thought to be more potent than the left for such a purpose;[6] and, this being the case, we may safely conclude that the use of both hands (as in the above-mentioned priestly blessing)[7] was

---

xxii. 26: cf. Prov. xi. 21, xvi. 5. Cf. the giving of the hand either in token of agreement or as a gesture of submission, 2 Kings x. 15; 1 Chron. xxix. 24; 2 Chron. xxx. 8; Ezra x. 19; Jer. l. 15; Lam. v. 6; Ezek. xvii. 18: also the idioms implying co-operation in Exod. xxiii. 1 (E); 1 Sam. xxii. 17; 2 Sam. iii. 12, xiv. 19; 2 Kings xv. 19; Ezra ix. 2; Jer. xxvi. 24; and (of God) 1 Chron. iv. 10.

[1] Gen. xiv. 22. Cf. (of God) Exod. vi. 8 (P); Num. xiv. 30 (P); Deut. xxxii. 40; Neh. ix. 15; Ps. cvi. 26; Ezek. xx. 5, 6, 15, 23, 28, 42, xxxvi. 7, xliv. 12, xlvii. 14: all, therefore, suggesting that the expression had become stereotyped and that to a certain extent at least the real significance of the gesture was not always appreciated. The right hand was, no doubt, usual (cf., perhaps, Isa. lxii. 8 (of God)); but one might employ both hands (cf. Dan. xii. 7).

[2] Gen. xxiv. 2, 9, xlvii. 29 (all J). Cf. the striking parallel quoted by G. J. Spurrell, *Notes on the Text of the Book of Genesis*, 2nd edit. rev. (1896), p. 218.

[3] Gen. xlviii. 8–22 (JE): cf. Num. xxvii. 18–23 (P); Deut. xxxiv. 9.

[4] Lev. ix. 22. [5] 2 Kings v. 11. [6] Gen. xlviii. 8–22 (JE).

[7] Lev. ix. 22: cf. Num. xxvii. 18–23 (P); Deut. xxxiv. 9. Brockington, of course, is right in his interpretation of the thought underlying the last two passages, when he says (op. cit., p. 193): 'Joshua was not only consecrated for leadership but also *equipped for it* by the laying on of Moses' hands.'

regarded as still more effective in achieving the desired end. Perhaps the most graphic illustration of the power thus thought to be mediated through the hands is that afforded by the account of Israel's victory over the Amalekites during the period of the Wandering, i.e.:[1]

And Amalek came and fought with Israel in Rephidim. And Moses said unto Joshua, Choose us out men, and go forth, fight against Amalek; tomorrow I will stand on the summit of the hill with the rod of God in my hand. So Joshua did as Moses told him with regard to fighting against Amalek, while Moses, Aaron, and Hur went up to the summit of the hill; and whenever Moses raised his hand aloft Israel would prevail, and whenever he lowered his hand Amalek would prevail. But Moses' hands were heavy; so they took a stone and placed it under him, and he sat down upon it, while Aaron and Hur supported his hands, the one on the one side and the other on the other. Thus his hands remained steady until sundown, and Joshua laid Amalek and his people low with the edge of the sword.

A similar example, which carries with it an added illustration of the power thought to be communicated through the actual touch of one's hand, is to be found in the story of Joash's visit to the dying Elisha, i.e.:[2]

Now when Elisha was sick of the sickness with which he was to die, Joash, king of Israel, went down to him, and wept over him, and said, My father! My father! The chariots and horsemen of Israel! And Elisha said to him, Take a bow and arrows; and he took to himself a bow and arrows. And he said to the king of Israel, Take the bow in hand; and when he had taken it in hand, Elisha laid his hands upon the king's hands. Then he said, Open the window towards the east; and he opened it. And Elisha said, Shoot; and he shot. And he said,

> Yahweh's arrow of victory!
> An arrow of victory over the Aramaeans!
> So shalt thou smite the Aramaeans in Aphek
> —*completely*!

Of course not everyone's hands were regarded as potent

---

[1] Exod. xvii. 8–13 (E): cf. the similar passages cited above, p. 56, n. 4.
[2] 2 Kings xiii. 14–17. Cf. in part 2 Kings iv. 34; and see further, with regard to the passage quoted in the text, *The Cultic Prophet in Ancient Israel*, p. 37, 2nd edit., p. 40.

in this way. As is clear from the passages cited, much depended upon individual circumstances and, in particular, one's relations with Yahweh; but this is an aspect of the question which lies outside our immediate field of inquiry.

The laying on of hands which is thus closely linked with the bestowal of blessing or the imparting of one's power in a magical or religio-magical way is to be distinguished (but not sharply distinguished) from such a cultic practice as that of making the worshipper lay his hand upon the head of an animal intended for sacrifice so as to associate himself with the victim;[1] and in this connexion one is reminded of the Deuteronomic idiom whereby stress is laid upon the worshipper's offering as his own personal gift by speaking of 'the heave offering of thy hand' or 'the free-will offering of thy hand'.[2] In fact, in this idiom, as in the case of the much more frequent and widespread references to 'the work of my (thy, his, &c.) hand(s)'[3] or even a passing reference to 'the work of thy fingers',[4] and

---

[1] Cf. (*a*) the burnt offering, Exod. xxix. 15 (P); Lev. i. 4, viii. 18; Num. viii. 12 (P): (*b*) the so-called peace-offering, Lev. iii. 2, 8, 13: (*c*) the sin-offering, Exod. xxix. 10 (P); Lev. iv. 4, 15, 24, 29, 33, viii. 14; Num. viii. 12 (P); 2 Chron. xxix. 23: (*d*) the ram used in the ritual of installation prescribed for the Aaronite priesthood, Exod. xxix. 19 (P); Lev. viii. 22: and even (*e*) the dedication of the Levites in terms of a wave-offering, Num. viii. 10 (P). Cf., too, the ritual associated with (i) the part played by the scapegoat in the ceremonies of the Day of Atonement, Lev. xvi. 21 (where emphasis is laid upon the use of the two hands); and (ii) the stoning of a blasphemer, Lev. xxiv. 14 (H).

[2] i.e. (*a*) Deut. xii. 17 (cf. verses 6 and 11): (*b*) Deut. xvi. 10. Cf. the similar idioms in (i) Deut. xv. 2: (ii) Deut. xvi. 17: (iii) Ezek. xlvi. 5, 11.

[3] Cf. the following representative passages: (*a*) of man, Deut. ii. 7, iv. 28, xiv. 29, xxvii. 15, xxxi. 29; 1 Kings xvi. 7; 2 Kings xix. 18, xxii. 17; 2 Chron. xxxii. 19; Job i. 10; Pss. xxviii. 4, xc. 17, cxv. 4; Eccles. v. 5 (EVV. 6); Song of Sol. vii. 2 (EVV. 1); Isa. ii. 8, xvii. 8, lxv. 22; Jer. i. 16, x. 9, xxv. 6 f.; Lam. iii. 64, iv. 2; Hos. xiv. 4 (EVV. 3); Mic. v. 12 (EVV. 13); Hag. ii. 14, 17; (*b*) of God, Job xiv. 15, xxxiv. 19; Pss. viii. 7 (EVV. 6), xix. 2 (EVV. 1), xcii. 5 (EVV. 4); Isa. v. 12, xix. 25, lxiv. 7 (EVV. 8).

[4] Ps. viii. 4 (EVV. 3), of God. Cf. (of man) Isa. ii. 8 and xvii. 8, as cited in the preceding note. These two passages are specially interesting, as they offer examples of what we may call progressive synecdoche! e.g. (to quote from the former): 'They bow down to the work of their hands, to what their fingers have made.'

the like,[1] we may recognize once more that partiality for synecdoche which we have already met in dealing with other parts of the body.

Indeed, this feature is to be found, not only in the use of the term for hand in simple nominal constructions such as the foregoing, but also (and more strikingly) in its frequent close association with verbal forms, whereby the hand itself is represented, not merely as the instrument of the *ego* (אֲנִי or אָנֹכִי), but as itself actively engaged in some form of personal behaviour, or as itself characterized by some personal quality. Thus, just as one may speak of 'the work of my hand(s)' and the like, so one may refer to the hand as being actually engaged in such an operation, as when the Preacher says (with a balance of clauses which should be noted):[2]

> Then I contemplated all my works that *my hands* had wrought and the labour that *I* had laboured to do.

In the same way the hand may be referred to with more precision as kissing one's mouth,[3] grasping an object[4] or leaving it alone,[5] cooking food,[6] bringing offerings,[7] engaged in building operations,[8] bearing rule,[9] effecting

---

[1] Cf. the idiom referred to above, p. 55, n. 4: and the similar expressions in (*a*) Isa. xxv. 11 (?): (*b*) Judges ix. 16; Prov. xii. 14; Isa. iii. 11: (*c*) Ps. lviii. 3 (EVV. 2): (*d*) Gen. xxxi. 42 (E); Ps. cxxviii. 2; Hag. i. 11; also (of God) Job x. 3; all with literal reference to the palm: (*e*) Gen. v. 29 (J): (*f*) Deut. xxxiii. 11; Ps. ix. 17 (EVV. 16); the latter with literal reference to the palm: (*g*) Prov. xxxi. 16, 31; the former with literal reference to the palm: (*h*) Ezek. xxvii. 15 (cf. verse 21): and (*i*) Jer. xxxiv. 1.

[2] Eccles. ii. 11. Cf. Job v. 12; Isa. xxxi. 7, lvi. 2: also (of God) Job xii. 9; Ps. cxviii. 15 f. (with specific reference to the right hand); Isa. xli. 20; and the passages dealing with His creative activity which are cited below, n. 8. Cf. also (with reference to the fingers) Isa. ii. 8 and xvii. 8, as cited above, p. 60, n. 4; and the suggestion of co-operation in the passages cited above, p. 57, n. 11, *ad fin.*   [3] Job xxxi. 27.

[4] Gen. xxv. 26 (J); 2 Sam. xxiii. 10: cf. (of God) Deut. xxxii. 41; Amos ix. 2. Similarly (of the right hand) 2 Sam. xx. 9; also (of God) Ps. cxxxix. 10.

[5] Deut. xv. 3.   [6] i.e. in the gruesome picture, Lam. iv. 10.

[7] Lev. vii. 30 (P).

[8] Zech. iv. 9. Cf. the references to Yahweh's creative activity in Exod. xv. 17 (J); Job x. 8; Pss. xcv. 5, cxix. 73; Isa. lxvi. 2; and (with specific reference to the right hand) Isa. xlviii. 13.

[9] Prov. xii. 24: cf. Jer. xxxiv. 1, as cited above, n. 1.

deliverance,[1] smiting someone[2] or making him homeless,[3] shedding blood,[4] and so on,[5] just as a man's opportunity or the extent of his power is indicated by reference to that which his hand may 'find'[6] or whatever it may 'reach'.[7]

In this way, too, the hand may be spoken of as becoming weary,[8] or as capable of being taught,[9] or even as refusing to act in a given situation;[10] and occasionally, like some of the other parts of the body which have already been discussed, it is subject to a moral judgement and so may be referred to in ethical terms. David, for example, in calling Saul's attention to the fact that he had spared his life when he had him at his mercy, says (again with a balance of clauses which should be noted):[11]

> There is no evil or rebellion *in my hand*, nor have *I* sinned against thee.

Sometimes the evil or iniquity thus associated with the hands is defined more closely, i.e. when the right hand is

---

[1] Judges vii. 2; 1 Sam. xxv. 26, 33. Similarly (of the right hand) Job xl. 14: also (of God) Pss. xliv. 4 (EVV. 3), xcviii. 1, cxxxviii. 7. Cf. (of Yahweh's help and protection) Ps. cxix. 173; Isa. xxv. 10.

[2] Joshua ii. 19; Job xx. 22; Zech. xiv. 13. Cf. (of God) 1 Sam. vi. 9 (cf. verse 3); Job xix. 21, xxvi. 13.

[3] Exod. xv. 9 (J); Ps. xxvi. 12 (EVV. 11).

[4] Deut. xxi. 7; Prov. vi. 17.

[5] Cf. Job xx. 10; Lam. iv. 6; Prov. x. 4 (with additional reference to the palm): also (of God) Job v. 18; Isa. xxxiv. 17. Similarly, with reference to the right hand (all of God): Exod. xv. 6 (J); Pss. xviii. 36 (EVV. 35), lxiii. 9 (EVV. 8), lxxviii. 54, lxxx. 16 (EVV. 15).

[6] Lev. xxv. 28 (H); Judges ix. 33; 1 Sam. x. 7, xxv. 8; Eccles. ix. 10. Cf. 1 Sam. xxiii. 17; Job xxxi. 25; Isa. x. 14; and (with specific reference to the right hand) Ps. xxi. 9 (EVV. 8): also (of God) Isa. x. 10.

[7] (*a*) Lev. v. 7 (P): (*b*) Lev. v. 11, xiv. 21, 22, 30, 31, 32 (all P), xxv. 26, 47, 49 (all H), xxvii. 8 (P); Num. vi. 21 (P); Ezek. xlvi. 7.

[8] 2 Sam. xxiii. 10.

[9] 2 Sam. xxii. 35 (= Ps. xviii. 35 (EVV. 34)); Ps. cxliv. 1. Cf. (with literal reference to the palm) Ps. lxxviii. 72: and (of the right hand) Pss. xlv. 5 (EVV. 4), cxxxvii. 5: also (of the arms) Hos. vii. 15.

[10] Prov. xxi. 25 (with which one may contrast xxxi. 13).

[11] 1 Sam. xxiv. 12 (EVV. 11). Cf. 1 Sam. xxvi. 18; Job xi. 14; Ps. xxvi. 10; Isa. xxxi. 7, lvi. 2; Ezek. xviii. 8: also (with literal reference to the palm) 1 Chron. xii. 18 (EVV. 17); Job xvi. 17, xxxi. 7; Ps. vii. 4 (EVV. 3); Isa. lix. 6; Jonah iii. 8; Mic. vii. 3 (cf. LXX): (with specific reference to the right hand) Ps. cxliv. 8, 11; Isa. xliv. 20: and (of the fingers) Isa. lix. 3.

described as being filled with a bribe,[1] or when both hands
are said to be filled with blood;[2] so that reference to the
'cleanness' of one's hands is idiomatic as a means of denoting one's state of innocence or one's positive righteousness.[3]

On the other hand, in many examples of the use of the
term under discussion its original force is largely lost; so
that, somewhat like the terms נֶפֶשׁ and פָּנִים, for example,
it is sometimes used with a suffix as little more than an
emphatic form of the personal pronoun. Thus, to say that
a thing is done 'from my hand' is simply to say that it is
done 'of myself' or 'by me';[4] and to say that a thing may be
required 'from thy hand' is simply an emphatic way of saying that it may be demanded 'of thee';[5] while to say of a
man that he brought something 'in (*or* with) his hand' may
mean no more than that he brought it 'with him'.[6] All in

---

[1] Ps. xxvi. 10: cf. (with literal reference to the palm) Isa. xxxiii. 15. Cf. also
the expression 'to fill the hand of' someone, which is used idiomatically of
installation into priestly office, i.e. Exod. xxviii. 41, xxix. 9, 29, 33, 35 (all P);
Lev. viii. 33, xvi. 32 (both P), xxi. 10 (H); Num. iii. 3 (P); Judges xvii. 5, 12;
1 Kings xiii. 33; 2 Chron. xiii. 9: cf. Exod. xxxii. 29 (J); 1 Chron. xxix. 5;
2 Chron. xxix. 31. The original force of this expression (which has something
of a parallel in 2 Kings ix. 24 and in the Accadian UMALLI ḴÂTA (ḴÂTÂ)) is
a matter of dispute: cf., for example, G. B. Gray, I.C.C. (1903), on Num.
iii. 3. It is clear, however, from its use in such an obviously early passage as
Judges xvii that it was an idiom of long standing; and, what is more, it must
ultimately have lost its original force, for it could even be used of installing
an altar, i.e. Ezek. xliii. 26. Cf. now M. Noth, *Amt und Berufung im Alten
Testament* (1958), pp. 7 ff. (= *Gesammelte Studien zum Alten Testament*,
2nd edit. enlarged (1960), pp. 311 ff.).

[2] Isa. i. 15. Cf. Ezek. xxiii. 37, 45: also (with literal reference to the palm)
Isa. lix. 3.

[3] 2 Sam. xxii. 21 (= Ps. xviii. 21 (EVV. 20)); Job xvii. 9; Ps. xviii. 25
(EVV. 24). Cf. (with literal reference to the palm) Gen. xx. 5 (E); Job xxii.
30; Ps. xxiv. 4: also Pss. xxvi. 6, lxxiii. 13. Note too in this connexion the rite
prescribed in Deut. xxi. 6 f. See also (with reference to the righteous activity
of God) Ps. xlviii. 11 (EVV. 10); Isa. xli. 10.

[4] Judges xvii. 3; Mal. i. 9; and (of God) Isa. l. 11 (cf. Gen. xlix. 24 (J)).

[5] Ezek. iii. 18, 20, xxxiii. 8: cf. 2 Sam. iv. 11; Isa. i. 12; Mal. i. 10, 13,
ii. 13.

[6] e.g. 1 Sam. xiv. 34; Jer. xxxviii. 11 (!): cf. EVV. Cf., too, the frequent
use of this term with the preposition בְּ (either in the construct state or with
a suffix) to denote agency or instrumentality in contexts which show that the
literal meaning is out of the question: e.g. Exod. ix. 35 (P); Lev. viii. 36 (P);
Num. iv. 37 (P); 1 Sam. xxviii. 15, 17; 1 Kings xii. 15; 1 Chron. xi. 3;

all, therefore, such idiomatic reference to the hand as we have discussed above, while often instructive, must not be over-emphasized. As already indicated, what we have here is again no more than that simple form of synecdoche whereby in certain circumstances an important part of one's נֶפֶשׁ or person, as being the temporary focus of attention, may be used picturesquely and graphically with reference to the individual as a whole. Thus there is nothing here to justify the conclusion that the Israelites thought in terms of a 'diffusion of consciousness'; but there is much to illustrate the Israelite conception of man as a psycho-physical organism and, what is more, the quite extra-ordinary importance of the hands as a measure of one's vitality or as a guide to one's mood, purpose, or character.[1]

The remaining peripheral parts of the body call for little if any consideration. We may note, however, that an 'out-stretched' neck (גָּרוֹן, צַוָּאר)[2] is a clear sign of pride or, as we say, that one is 'stuck up', while it is idiomatic to speak of a 'stiff' neck (עֹרֶף)[3] or a 'rebellious' shoulder

2 Chron. xxix. 25 (also of God); Ezra ix. 11; Neh. ix. 30; Isa. xx. 2; Jer. xxxvii. 2; Ezek. xxxviii. 17; Hag. i. 1; Zech. vii. 12; Mal. i. 1; and so often: also 2 Kings xix. 23; Esther i. 12; Isa. lxiv. 6 (EVV. 7); Jer. xxxix. 11, &c. Cf. also the renderings of the standard English versions in such passages as Judges iii. 15; 1 Sam. xvi. 20; 1 Kings x. 29; 2 Chron. vii. 6, xxiv. 13.

[1] See below, p. 81, n. 5; and in this connexion note too the significance of the grammatical construction, characteristic of elevated style, whereby the word for 'hand' may be introduced in the nominative case along with a purely personal subject to denote the organ employed in performing the given action, i.e. Deut. xxxiii. 7; and (of God) Pss. xvii. 14, xliv. 3 (EVV. 2); Isa. xlv. 12: also (of the right hand) Ps. lx. 7 (EVV. 5) = cviii. 7 (EVV. 6); Lam. ii. 4 (all of God). Cf. p. 45, n. 1, on the similar use of the term for 'mouth': and see further G.K., § 144*lm*; G. R. Driver, in *The People and the Book*, ed. A. S. Peake (1925), pp. 117 f.

[2] Ps. lxxv. 6 (EVV. 5); Isa. iii. 16 (vide G. B. Gray, I.C.C. (1912), *in loc.*): cf. Job xv. 26.

[3] Exod. xxxii. 9, xxxiii. 3, 5, xxxiv. 9 (all J or JE); Deut. ix. 6, 13, x. 16, xxxi. 27; 2 Kings xvii. 14; 2 Chron. xxx. 8, xxxvi. 13; Neh. ix. 16, 17, 29; Prov. xxix. 1; Jer. vii. 26, xvii. 23, xix. 15: cf. Isa. xlviii. 4. Despite the apparent parallel in the fairly frequent metaphorical reference to one's 'horn' as being 'lifted up' like that of the wild ox (Ps. xcii. 11 (EVV. 10), &c.), and the gnashing or grinding of the teeth (cf. Job xvi. 9; Pss. xxxv. 16, xxxvii. 12, cxii. 10; Lam. ii. 16), it seems to the writer that the last of the foregoing passages and the similar idioms in respect of other parts of the body do

(כָּתֵף)[1] as an indication of obstinacy. On the other hand, of course, to do something 'with one shoulder' (שְׁכֶם), i.e., as we might say, to unite in putting one's back into it, is to make a united effort or undertake a common task.[2] Further, trembling knees (sing.: בֶּרֶךְ) are an obvious sign not only of sheer physical weakness,[3] but of despondency[4] or utter panic,[5] while there is a clear instance of synecdoche in the description of the seven thousand faithful adherents of Yahweh as:[6]

All the knees which have not bowed down to the Baal, and all the mouths which have not kissed him.

Indeed this example of synecdoche has an exact parallel in the triumphant claim voiced by the great prophet of the Exile on behalf of Yahweh:[7]

> To Me every knee shall bow,
> By Me every tongue shall swear.

Similarly the action of the foot (רֶגֶל), as in being stamped, may be eloquent of malice or exultant satisfaction,[8] while the practice of placing one's foot on the neck of a defeated

---

not favour the view that 'the figure is of an animal refusing to turn in the direction his rider desires'. G. A. Smith, C.B. (1918), on Deut. ix. 6: cf. S. R. Driver, I.C.C., 3rd edit. (1902), *in loc.* Cf. rather C. H. Toy, I.C.C. (1899), on Prov. xxix. 1, i.e.: 'Stiffening the neck, in obstinate persistence, is the opposite of bending the neck in token of submission.'

[1] Neh. ix. 29; Zech. vii. 11. Here again it seems to the writer that the similar idioms in respect of other parts of the body militate against the view that 'the figure is taken from an animal which will submit to no yoke upon its neck'. S. R. Driver, Cent.B. (1906), on Zech. vii. 11: cf. H. E. Ryle, C.B. (1893), on Neh. ix. 29.

[2] Cf. Zeph. iii. 9, which should be read in the light of (*a*) Job xxxi. 36; Isa. ix. 5, xxii. 22 (rather than Gen. xlix. 15 (J), unless the parallelism points to an abandonment of the simile; Isa. x. 27, xiv. 25): (*b*) Jer. xxxii. 39; Ezek. xi. 19.

[3] Cf. Ps. cix. 24.

[4] Job iv. 4; Isa. xxxv. 3.

[5] Ezek. vii. 17, xxi. 12 (EVV. 7); Nahum ii. 11 (EVV. 10).

[6] 1 Kings xix. 18.

[7] Isa. xlv. 23. Contrast 1 Kings viii. 54; 2 Chron. vi. 13; Ezra ix. 5: also Judges vii. 5, 6; 2 Kings i. 13.

[8] Ezek. vi. 11, xxv. 6: cf. Prov. vi. 13.

foe provided an obvious symbol of triumph and power.[1]
It is no matter for surprise, therefore, that the term for foot
should sometimes be employed by synecdoche to denote the
individual as a whole; and a simple illustration of this may
be found in Saul's instructions to the Ziphites with regard
to the whereabouts of David, i.e.:[2]

> Go now, ascertain once more, and know and see his place where his
> foot may be.

In fact the foot may be referred to in this way as if it were
itself engaged in some form of personal activity or behaviour,
as when the psalmist prays:[3]

> Let not the foot of pride come upon me,
> Nor the hand of the wicked make me a wanderer.

This corresponds to the way in which the foot is spoken
of, not merely as coming and going or the like (as in the
preceding quotation),[4] but as treading or trampling,[5] taking
its stand[6] or slipping,[7] and even in one picturesque instance

---

[1] Joshua x. 24. Cf. the metaphor of Ps. cx. 1: also the similar implications
in 2 Sam. xxii. 39 (= Ps. xviii. 39 (EVV. 38)); Pss. viii. 7 (EVV. 6), xlvii. 4
(EVV. 3); Lam. iii. 34; and (of the soles of the feet) 1 Kings v. 17 (EVV. 3);
Mal. iii. 21 (EVV. iv. 3).

[2] 1 Sam. xxiii. 22. Cf. (of God) Isa. lx. 13; Ezek. xliii. 7: i.e. corresponding
to the explicit references to the Ark, Temple, or Earth as Yahweh's 'footstool'
in 1 Chron. xxviii. 2; Pss. xcix. 5, cxxxii. 7; Isa. lxvi. 1; Lam. ii. 1.

[3] Ps. xxxvi. 12 (EVV. 11).

[4] Cf. the various verbs employed in the following passages: (a) 1 Kings
xiv. 12; Job xxiii. 11, xxxi. 5; Ps. xxxvi. 12 (EVV. 11); Prov. i. 16, v. 5, vi.
18; Isa. xxiii. 7, lix. 7; Ezek. xxix. 11: (b) less forcefully, 2 Kings xxi. 8 (cf.
2 Chron. xxxiii. 8); Ps. cxix. 59; Prov. iv. 27, xxv. 17; Isa. lviii. 13; Jer. xiv.
10: and (c) Isa. xxxii. 20 (of domestic animals) as compared with Job xxx. 12.
Cf., too, Prov. iv. 26: and the idiom of Gen. xxx. 30 (J); Job xviii. 11; Isa.
xli. 2.

[5] (a) Joshua xiv. 9: and (of the sole of the foot) Deut. ii. 5, xi. 24; Joshua
i. 3: (b) Isa. xxvi. 6: cf. xxviii. 3; Ezek. xxxiv. 19 (as against verse 18).

[6] Pss. xxvi. 12, cxxii. 2; and (of God) Zech. xiv. 4. Cf. (a) of the soles of the
feet, Joshua iii. 13 (corresponding to iv. 3, 9); also Deut. xxviii. 65 and (of
a dove) Gen. viii. 9 (J): (b) Prov. vii. 11. See also Pss. xxxi. 9 (EVV. 8), xl. 3
(EVV. 2), as cited below, p. 67, n. 4.

[7] (a) Deut. xxxii. 35; Pss. xxxviii. 17 (EVV. 16), lxvi. 9, lxxiii. 2 (Q), xciv.
18, cxxi. 3: (b) Prov. xxv. 19 (*Qal*): (c) Jer. xiii. 16. Cf. Pss. lvi. 14 (EVV. 13),
cxvi. 8: also (of the ankles) 2 Sam. xxii. 37 = Ps. xviii. 37 (EVV. 36).

as being forgetful (i.e. of the miner's unfamiliar haunts).[1]
Sometimes, of course, the language is purely metaphorical.
If one is involved in trouble, for example, one may employ
a hunting metaphor and speak of having the foot caught in
a snare,[2] while the slipping of the foot furnishes an equally
clear metaphor to denote calamity or even loss of faith.[3]
On the other hand, again, deliverance from trouble may be
described as having one's feet stationed 'in a broad place'
or as having them set 'upon the rock' (i.e. on firm ground).[4]
Similarly one may speak of the foot as hastening towards
evil[5] or, on the other hand, as being turned away from evil
in the direction of Yahweh's laws.[6] In fact, to keep one's
foot planted firmly on this road is an indication of one's
integrity, as Job reveals when he says (with yet another
balance of clauses which should be noted):[7]

> *My foot* hath held fast to His steps;
> His way have *I* kept, and not turned aside.

All in all, therefore, whether the language be metaphorical
or not, the style of speech is familiar and the presence of
synecdoche perfectly obvious; and, once more, there is
nothing in such language to warrant the theory of a 'diffused
consciousness' in the associated conception of man.[8]

Further, the conception of man as a psycho-physical
organism can be seen equally clearly in the use of the terminology for the internal parts of the body. Despondency,
for example, is felt to have a shrivelling effect upon the
bones (sing.: עֶצֶם),[9] just as they are said to decay or become

---

[1] Job xxviii. 4.

[2] (a) Job xviii. 8; Pss. ix. 16 (EVV. 15), xxv. 15; Lam. i. 13: (b) Jer. xviii. 22. Cf. Job xiii. 27, xxxiii. 11.

[3] (a) Deut. xxxii. 35; Job xii. 5; Pss. xxxviii. 17 (EVV. 16), lvi. 14 (EVV. 13), lxvi. 9, xciv. 18, cxvi. 8, cxxi. 3; Jer. xiii. 16: (b) Ps. lxxiii. 2 (Q).

[4] Pss. xxxi. 9 (EVV. 8), xl. 3 (EVV. 2): cf. 1 Sam. ii. 9; Prov. iii. 26.

[5] Prov. i. 16, vi. 18; Isa. lix. 7: cf. Job xxxi. 5.

[6] Ps. cxix. 59, 101; Prov. iv. 27. Cf. Prov. i. 15; also Isa. lviii. 13.

[7] Job xxiii. 11: cf. Eccles. iv. 17 (EVV. v. 1).

[8] See below, p. 81, n. 5.

[9] Ezek. xxxvii. 11: cf. Prov. xvii. 22, as below, p. 68, n. 9.

soft with fear or distress,[1] and so may be referred to as being themselves troubled or afraid.[2] Similarly they may be described as virtually aflame with one's conflicting thoughts[3] or breaking up under the gnawing action of jealousy,[4] while words spoken in mockery or as a curse are regarded as having so penetrative a power that (in a far more realistic way than that of the soft tongue which breaks down one's resistance)[5] they can cause the bones to disintegrate and collapse.[6] On the other hand, their marrow is felt to be enriched and their vigour restored when the hearer is the recipient of good tidings or pleasant words,[7] and in such a case may actually be said to exult in and of themselves.[8] Indeed they are seen to form so fundamental a part of man's being that they provide an obvious parallel to the term נֶפֶשׁ, when this denotes the whole personality conceived as functioning psychically; so that a suppliant of Yahweh, having begun his prayer with a plea for the destruction of his enemies, can continue:[9]

---

[1] Hab. iii. 16; Jer. xxiii. 9: cf. Pss. xxxi. 11 (EVV. 10), xxxii. 3, xxxviii. 4 (EVV. 3), cii. 4, 6 (EVV. 3, 5).

[2] Ps. vi. 3 (EVV. 2); Job iv. 14.   [3] Jer. xx. 9: cf. Lam. i. 13.

[4] Prov. xiv. 30.   [5] Cf. Prov. xxv. 15 (as below, n. 9).

[6] Pss. xlii. 11 (EVV. 10), cix. 18: cf. xxii. 15, 18 (EVV. 14, 17); Lam. iii. 4; and bear in mind such a passage as Num. v. 11–31 (P).

[7] Prov. xv. 30, xvi. 24 (but see below, n. 9): cf. Job xxi. 24; Prov. iii. 8; Isa. lviii. 11, lxvi. 14.

[8] Ps. li. 10 (EVV. 8).

[9] Ps. xxxv. 9 f. Cf. the association of these terms in Job vii. 15 (retaining the reading of M.T. as against most moderns, e.g. Driver–Gray, I.C.C. (1921), and Dhorme, E.B. (1926)); Ps. vi. 3 f. (EVV. 2 f.); Prov. xvi. 24; Isa. lviii. 11: but see also with regard to the first of these passages (and, perhaps, Job iv. 14, as above, n. 2) G. R. Driver, in *E.T.* lvii (1945–6), p. 193. In Lam. iv. 7 the singular (עֶצֶם) is used with the force of 'body' (cf. the consonantal text of Ps. cxxxix. 15; also perhaps Prov. xv. 30 and xvi. 24, as above, n. 7); and this is in line with its metaphorical use in reinforcing an allusion, i.e. so as to say 'like the sky itself' (Exod. xxiv. 10 (J)) or 'this very day' (Gen. vii. 13 (P); Ezek. xxiv. 2, &c.). In Job xxi. 23 it may be taken in either a literal or a metaphorical sense with much the same result, although the latter is the one which is usually favoured: cf. again Driver–Gray and Dhorme, as above. Note also that in post-Biblical Hebrew it is used with the appropriate suffixes to refer to 'myself', 'thyself', &c.: cf. the illustration from modern Hebrew which is given below, p. 75, n. 5, *ad fin.* Finally, the singular term גֶּרֶם, which is rare in classical Hebrew (vide Prov. xvii. 22 and xxv. 15,

Then I myself shall rejoice in Yahweh;
I shall exult in His salvation.
(*lit.* Then my נֶפֶשׁ will rejoice in Yahweh;
It will exult in His salvation.)
All my bones will say:
Yahweh, who is like unto Thee?

Finally, if it be borne in mind that men are also seen to vary in their degree of vital power, one can readily understand the statement that after the death of Elisha (an exceptionally forceful personality) mere contact with his bones was sufficient to reanimate a corpse.[1]

Like the bones, the blood (דָּם) also provides a close parallel to the term נֶפֶשׁ; for, as we have already noticed, it is described as being or containing the נֶפֶשׁ as the life-principle, and indeed may be used accordingly with a quite general reference to denote the common life which is shared by man with other living creatures.[2] Indeed the obviously vital significance of blood gave it a place of first importance in the ritual of the cultus as the professional way of maintaining right relationship with Yahweh in His role as the Giver of Life.[3] In fact all blood is taboo for man, so that even in the case of animal food it may not be consumed, but must be reserved in a sacrificial manner for Yahweh Himself;[4] and even the slaughter of human beings in the form of the nation's foes appears to have been envisaged at

as cited above, p. 67, n. 9, and p. 68, n. 5), has much the same general force, and appears to be used in a similar metaphorical way in 2 Kings ix. 13: cf., too, the cognate Aramaic term גַּרְמָא (Syriac ܓܰܪܡܳܐ), which is also employed with the appropriate suffixes to refer to 'myself', 'thyself', &c.

[1] 2 Kings xiii. 20 f.

[2] Gen. ix. 4–6 (P); Lev. xvii. 10–14 (H); Deut. xii. 23–25; as above, p. 9, n. 1. Cf., too, the parallelism of such passages as Ps. lxxii. 14; Prov. i. 18.

[3] e.g. Exod. xii. 1–13 (P), 21–27 (J), xxiii. 18 (E), xxiv. 3–8 (E), xxix. 1–xxx. 10 (P), xxxiv. 25 (J); Lev. i, iii–ix, xiv, xvi (all P), xvii (H); Num. xviii. 17 (P), xix. 4 f. (P); Deut. xii. 13–28, xv. 19–23; 1 Sam. xiv. 31 ff.; 2 Kings xvi. 10–18; 2 Chron. xxix. 20 ff., xxx. 13 ff.; Ps. l. 13; Isa. i. 11, xxxiv. 6 f.; Ezek. xxxix. 17 ff., xliii. 18 ff., xliv. 7, 15 f., xlv. 18 ff.; Zech. ix. 11.

[4] Cf. Gen. ix. 4 (P); Lev. iii. 17, vii. 26 f. (both P), xvii. 10–14, xix. 26 (both H); Deut. xii. 16, 23–25, xv. 23; 1 Sam. xiv. 31 ff.; Ezek. xxxiii. 25; Zech. ix. 7.

one time as a kind of sacrifice requiring definite cultic safe-guards.[1] What is more, reference is often made to violent death in terms of shedding blood,[2] and this is frequently described in such a way as to reveal an undercurrent of fascination, whether that of horror or exultant satisfaction.[3] Indeed the simple term דָּם is often used symbolically of such violent or premature death; and this is especially true of the plural דָּמִים, which is employed by itself to denote not only shed blood but even the guilt arising from such bloodshed.[4] Hence any shedding of blood from within or

---

[1] War was normally regarded as a sacred activity. It was begun with an act of consecration (cf. Jer. vi. 4; Joel iv. 9 (EVV. iii. 9), Mic. iii. 5), which included the offering of sacrifice (e.g. 1 Sam. vii. 9, xiii. 8 ff.; Ps. xx); and there is some indication that, originally at least, the participants, as being consecrated to the task (Isa. xiii. 3: cf. Jer. xxii. 7, li. 27 f.), were expected to abstain from sexual intercourse during the campaign (cf. 1 Sam. xxi. 5 f. (EVV. 4 f.); 2 Sam. xi. 11 ff.). Cf., too, the use of √חרם in this connexion, e.g. in Deut. vii with its theory of the conquest of Canaan in terms of a חֵרֶם (A.V. usually 'accursed thing': R.V., R.S.V. usually 'devoted thing'), noting that, as seems clear from the corresponding Arabic √حرم, as in حُرْم, 'to be forbidden', حَرَام, 'forbidden' or 'sacred', and حَرِيم, 'harem', the verbal form הֶחֱרִים (EVV., R.S.V. usually 'utterly destroy': R.V. mgn. 'Heb. devote') really means 'to render taboo' or 'to make sacred', and, therefore, in certain contexts almost literally 'to sacrifice'. Cf. also the pictorial language of Isa. xxxiv. 5 ff. (including the use of the term חֵרֶם in verse 5), Jer. xlvi. 10, and Ezek. xxxix. 17 ff.

[2] e.g. Gen. ix. 6 (P), xxxvii. 22 (J); Num. xxxv. 33 (P); Deut. xix. 10, xxi. 7; 1 Sam. xxv. 31; 1 Kings ii. 31; 2 Kings xxiv. 4; 1 Chron. xxii. 8, xxviii. 3; Pss. lxxix. 3, 10, cvi. 38; Prov. i. 16, vi. 17; Jer. vii. 6, xxii. 3, 17; Lam. iv. 13; Ezek. xvi. 38, xviii. 10, xxii. 3, 4, 6, 9, 12, 27, xxiii. 45, xxxvi. 18; Zeph. i. 17.

[3] e.g. Num. xxiii. 24 (E); Deut. xxxii. 42; 2 Sam. i. 22, xx. 12; 1 Kings xxi. 19, xxii. 35, 38; 2 Kings ix. 33; Ps. lviii. 11 (EVV. 10); Isa. xv. 9, xxxiv. 3, 6, 7, xlix. 26; Jer. xlvi. 10, xlviii. 10; Ezek. xxxix. 17 ff. Cf., too, the passages cited in the following notes: and (a) Lev. xii, xv. 19–30 (both P), xx. 18 (H); Ezek. xvi. 6, 9, 22; (b) Joel iii. 3 f. (EVV. ii. 30 f.).

[4] Cf. (a) for the *singular* of the noun with the implication of violent or premature death, Gen. xlii. 22 (J); Deut. xvii. 8; Joshua ii. 19; Judges ix. 24; 2 Sam. iii. 27, iv. 11; 1 Kings ii. 9, 32, 37; 2 Chron. xix. 10; Prov. i. 11, 18, xii, 6; Ezek. v. 17, xxi. 37 (EVV. 32), xxiii. 37, 45, xxiv. 7 f., xxviii. 23, xxxiii. 4 f., xxxv. 6, xxxviii. 22; Hos. vi. 8, &c.: (b) for the *plural* of the noun with the implication of violent or premature death, Gen. iv. 10 f. (J); Lev. xx. 9, 11 ff. (H); 2 Sam. iii. 28, xvi. 8; 1 Kings ii. 5, 31, 33; 2 Kings ix. 7, 26; 2 Chron. xxiv. 25; Ps. ix. 13 (EVV. 12); Isa. i. 15, iv. 4, xxvi. 21, xxxiii. 15; Ezek. vii. 23, ix. 9, xvi. 36, xviii. 13; Hos. i. 4, iv. 2; Mic. iii. 10, vii. 2; Hab.

without the social unit is a responsible matter involving some form of retaliation.[1] Within the nation itself, for example, the individual's responsibility for the life of his fellow Israelite is conceived as the protecting of his blood;[2] and it is legally recognized that wilful murder, as distinct from simple manslaughter,[3] involves a shedding of blood which must be made good on the principle of the *lex talionis*.[4] Accordingly it is a matter for serious concern when the blood which is shed is that of an inoffensive individual; and it is wholly in line with what we have already observed concerning the employment of synecdoche that in such a

ii. 8, 12, 17, &c.: (c) for the *plural* of the noun with reference to the guilt of bloodshed, Exod. xxii. 1 f. (EVV. 2 f.) (E); Deut. xix. 10, xxii. 8; 1 Sam. xxv. 26, 33; Ps. li. 16 (EVV. 14) (?); Hos. xii. 15 (EVV. 14): and its use as an epexegetical genitive to denote a man or a city regarded as 'guilty of' or 'prone to' such bloodshed, i.e. (i) 2 Sam. xvi. 7, 8; Pss. v. 7 (EVV. 6), xxvi. 9, lv. 24 (EVV. 23), lix. 3 (EVV. 2), cxxxix. 19; Prov. xxix. 10: (ii) Ezek. xxii. 2, xxiv. 6, 9; Nahum iii. 1. Cf. with regard to the last point the similar suggestion of responsibility in Exod. iv. 25 f. (J). See also in general (but with caution) G.K., § 124*n*.

[1] Cf. (a) in general, Gen. iv. 10 f. (J), ix. 5 f. (P); Joshua ii. 19: (b) of the shedding of Israelite blood by outsiders, Deut. xxxii. 43; 2 Sam. i. 16 (cf. verse 13); Pss. ix. 13 (EVV. 12), lxxix. 10; Jer. li. 35: (c) for the shedding of Israelite blood from within the social unit, Gen. xxxvii. 22 (E), 26 (J), xlii. 22 (E); Lev. xix. 16 (H); Judges ix. 23 f.; 2 Sam. iii. 27 f., iv. 11; 1 Kings ii. 31–33; 2 Kings ix. 7, 26; 2 Chron. xxiv. 25; Hos. i. 4; and the passages cited below, n. 4.

[2] Cf. Ezek. iii. 18, 20, xxxiii. 6, 8: also 2 Sam. xxiii. 17; 1 Chron. xi. 19.

[3] Cf. (i) Deut. xvii. 8; 2 Chron. xix. 10: and (ii) Exod. xxi. 12–14 (E); Num. xxxv. 16–23 (P); Deut. xix. 4–6, 11–13.

[4] The reference, of course, is to the form of גְּאֻלָּה which is admitted in Num. xxxv. 9–34 (P); Deut. xix. 1–13; Joshua xx (P): cf. 2 Sam. xiv. 11. Incidentally it may be pointed out that in the present writer's opinion √גאל, as it appears in the expression גְּאֻלָּה and corresponding forms, is basically the same as √גאל which occurs (e.g. in the verb *Niph'al*, *Pi'ēl*, &c.) with the implication of defilement; in short, both sets of ideas appear to stem from a root with the primary meaning 'to cover'. That is to say, we have here another example of semantic polarization (see above, p. 22, n. 3), so that in the one case the dominant idea is that of covering as means of 'protection' (with the possible further implication of 'redemption' in certain contexts), and, in the other case, that of covering as a form of 'defilement'. Thus in the passages under discussion the expression גֹּאֵל הַדָּם refers to the 'protector' of the blood of the kin-group rather than the 'avenger' of the shed blood (cf. EVV., R.S.V.). See further the writer's paper, 'The Primary Meaning of √גאל', in *Congress Volume: Copenhagen 1953*, S.V.T. i (1953), pp. 67–77.

case one should speak of shedding 'innocent blood'.[1] What is more (and here we have something of a parallel to that which we have noticed in the case of the bones), after death such shed blood is thought to retain a measure of psychical power in that it may continue to call for retaliation so long as it lies exposed to the public gaze. Thus, had Joseph's brothers murdered him, they would have been forced to conceal his blood; otherwise it would have cried out for vengeance against them, as the blood of the murdered Abel cried out against Cain.[2] Similarly Job, convinced that all his undeserved suffering is about to culminate in death, determines that his protest shall not be silenced by this dissolution of his personality; it shall continue to be voiced through his blood:[3]

> Earth, cover not my blood,
> And let there be no stay for my cry!

That is to say, it continues to make itself heard until such time as it is covered over either by human beings or by the fact that the soil has absorbed it;[4] and even then, if still unavenged, it is thought to continue its activity, being found capable of polluting the land and thereby interfering disastrously with the fertility of the soil and the general well-being of the State.[5]

---

[1] Deut. xix. 10, xxi. 8 f., xxvii. 25; 1 Sam. xix. 5; 2 Kings xxi. 16, xxiv. 4b; Pss. xciv. 21, cvi. 38; Prov. vi. 17; Isa. lix. 7; Jer. vii. 6, xxii. 3, xxvi. 15; Joel iv. 19 (EVV. iii. 19); Jonah i. 14. Cf. Deut. xix. 13; 2 Kings xxiv. 4a; Prov. i. 11; Jer. ii. 34, xix. 4, xxii. 17; Joel iv. 21 (EVV. iii. 21): also Lam. iv. 13. Note incidentally that in Prov. i. 11 there is no need to emend לְדָם ('for blood') to לְתָם ('for the perfect'), as is now commonly done: cf., for example, G. Wildeboer, K.H.C. (1897), C. H. Toy, I.C.C. (1899), C. Steuernagel, *H.S.A.T.* (1923), H. Wiesman, H.S.A.T. (1923), W. O. E. Oesterley, W.C. (1929), B. Gemser, H.A.T., 2nd edit. rev. (1963). The author has merely adopted the simple literary device of taking a familiar compound expression (in this case דָּם נָקִי, 'innocent blood') and using the first element of the Hebrew in the one stichos and the second element of the Hebrew in the following stichos.

[2] Gen. xxxvii. 22 (E), 26 (J), xlii. 22 (E): cf. iv. 10 f. (J).   [3] xvi. 18.

[4] Cf. (in addition to the foregoing examples) 1 Sam. xxvi. 20; 1 Kings ii. 31–33; Isa. xxvi. 21; Ezek. xxiv. 7 f.

[5] Cf. Num. xxxv. 9–34, esp. verse 33 (P); Deut. xxi. 1–9; 2 Sam. xxi. 1 (cf. LXX); Ps. cvi. 38.

Of the more central parts of the body the belly (בֶּטֶן) calls for mention in virtue of its obvious connexion with the digestive organs,[1] and its resultant usefulness as a figure for greed;[2] but still more important is its association with man's virility[3] and a woman's reproductive organs, particularly the womb (רֶחֶם).[4] Moreover, it is referred to occasionally as the scene of profound emotional disturbance[5] and even as concealing one's basic motives.[6] Accordingly it is no matter for surprise that it, too, should be used by synecdoche to denote the body as a whole.[7] Much the same is true of the loins (מָתְנַיִם, less often חֲלָצַיִם), which yield support for a loin-cloth or belt[8] and thus serve for the girding up of one's robe when speedy action or concentration of effort is

---

[1] Prov. xiii. 25: cf. Ps. xvii. 14; Prov. xviii. 20; Ezek. iii. 3.

[2] Cf. Job xx. 15, 20, 23.

[3] Ps. cxxxii. 11; Mic. vi. 7: cf. Deut. vii. 13, xxviii. 4, 11, 18, 53, xxx. 9. In Job xix. 17 the reference is uncertain. If Job's offspring be intended, it should be included here; but if the reference be to his brothers (cf. the language of iii. 10), this passage must be classed with those in the following note.

[4] Cf. (*a*) in general, Gen. xxv. 23 f. (J), xxx. 2 (E), xxxviii. 27 (J); Judges xiii. 5, 7, xvi. 17; Job i. 21, iii. 10, xxxi. 18, xxxviii. 29; Pss. xxii. 10 (EVV. 9), lxxi. 6, cxxvii. 3, cxxxix. 13; Prov. xxxi. 2; Eccles. v. 14 (EVV. 15), xi. 5; Isa. xiii. 18, xliv. 2, 24, xlviii. 8, xlix. 1, 5, 15; Hos. ix. 11, 16, xii. 4 (EVV. 3): (*b*) in close association with the term רֶחֶם, Job iii. 11, x. 18 f., xxxi. 15; Pss. xxii. 11 (EVV. 10), lviii. 4 (EVV. 3); Isa. xlvi. 3; Jer. i. 5.

[5] Job xxxii. 18 f. (cf. xv. 2); Hab. iii. 16. Cf. the close connexion between רֶחֶם and רַחֲמִים ('compassion'), although in this case one must beware of over-emphasizing the physical associations of the latter term, as appears to be done by Koeberle, op. cit., pp. 191 f.; Dhorme, *L'Emploi métaphorique, &c.*, pp. 134 f.; Eichrodt, op. cit., ii, p. 74, ii–iii, 4th edit., p. 95.

[6] Prov. xviii. 8, xx. 27, 30, xxii. 18, xxvi. 22: cf. Job xv. 35. There appears to be a corresponding use of the term קֶרֶב, i.e. with reference to one's 'inside'; but, as a matter of fact, in almost every instance the term in question occurs in its familiar use as a part of the prepositional phrase meaning 'within' (e.g. 1 Kings iii. 28; Pss. lxii. 5 (EVV. 4), xciv. 19; and so on). This being the case, it is almost negligible in the present connexion. The only passages which merit special mention are Pss. v. 10 (EVV. 9), lxiv. 7 (EVV. 6), ciii. 1; Isa. xvi. 11. In Ps. xlix. 12 (EVV. 11), if not in lxiv. 7 (EVV. 6), the text is doubtful: cf. LXX.

[7] Ps. xliv. 26 (EVV. 25): cf. Ps. xxxi. 10 (EVV. 9); Prov. xviii. 20.

[8] Cf. 2 Sam. xx. 8; 1 Kings ii. 5; 2 Kings i. 8; Neh. iv. 12 (EVV. 18); Job xii. 18; Isa. v. 27, xi. 5, xlv. 1; Jer. xiii. 1 f., 4, 11; Ezek. ix. 2, 3, 11, xxiii. 15; Dan. x. 5.

needed.[1] This, of course, corresponds to the fact that the loins are recognized as being the source of a man's strength[2] and procreative power,[3] and are found subject to a feeling of complete collapse in a situation which gives cause for agitation or apprehension.[4] What is more they, too, may engage one's attention in such a way as to lead to the employment of synecdoche, as when Job is made to protest that he never saw any man in need of clothing,[5]

> Except his loins blessed me,
> And he warmed himself with the fleece of my lambs.

For the rest, the bosom (חֵיק) is referred to in one instance as subject to feelings of vexation;[6] but on the whole (and somewhat surprisingly) it does not figure at all prominently in this connexion.[7]

In fact, as one might expect, it is in the terminology for the actual organs associated with the foregoing parts of the body that the Israelite conception of man as a psycho-physical organism finds most ready and frequent illustration. Thus the bowels (מֵעִים) are found to be stirred with feelings of love,[8] sympathy,[9] or despair,[10] while the kidneys or reins (כְּלָיוֹת) reveal similar extremes of emotional dis-

---

[1] Exod. xii. 11 (P); 1 Kings xviii. 46; 2 Kings iv. 29, ix. 1; Job xxxviii. 3, xl. 7; Prov. xxxi. 17; Jer. i. 17.

[2] Cf. Deut. xxxiii. 11; Ps. lxvi. 11 (?); Nahum ii. 2 (EVV. 1): also (a) 1 Kings xii. 10 = 2 Chron. x. 10: (b) Job xl. 16.

[3] Gen. xxxv. 11 (P); 1 Kings viii. 19 = 2 Chron. vi. 9.

[4] Ezek. xxi. 11 (EVV. 6): cf. Ps. lxix. 24 (EVV. 23); Isa. xxi. 3; Jer. xxx. 6; Ezek. xxix. 7; Nahum ii. 11 (EVV. 10).

[5] Job xxxi. 20. The readiness for such synecdoche may be seen by consulting (a) the allusions to the loin-cloth or girdle in the passages cited above, p. 73, n. 8: (b) the regulations concerning the priestly garments in Exod. xxviii. 42 (P); Ezek. xliv. 18: (c) the references to the use of sackcloth (usually as a sign of mourning or humiliation) in Gen. xxxvii. 34 (J); 1 Kings xx. 31 f.; Isa. xx. 2; Jer. xlviii. 37; Amos viii. 10: cf. Isa. xxxii. 11.

[6] Eccles. vii. 9.

[7] Note, however, the somewhat loose use of the term in Job xix. 27 (if the text be sound) and the figurative language of Pss. xxxv. 13, lxxxix. 51 (EVV. 50).

[8] Song of Sol. v. 4: cf. Ps. xl. 9 (EVV. 8).

[9] Isa. xvi. 11: cf. (of God) Isa. lxiii. 15; Jer. xxxi. 20.

[10] Jer. iv. 19; Lam. i. 20, ii. 11: cf. Job xxx. 27; Ps. xxii. 15 (EVV. 14).

turbance in being said, on the one hand, to exult,[1] and, on the other, to be weak with longing,[2] or the centre of acute concern.[3] Indeed the reins form so vital and so sensitive a part of the body[4] that in a measure it is here, concealed from one's fellow creatures if not from God, that the real sentiments of the elusive *ego* (אֲנִי or אָנֹכִי) find their expression.[5]

By far the most important organ, however, is the heart (לֵב, לֵבָב), which obtains mention even more frequently than the wide-ranging term נֶפֶשׁ.[6] Its actual physiological

---

[1] Prov. xxiii. 16.   [2] Job xix. 27.   [3] Ps. lxxiii. 21.

[4] Cf. Job xvi. 13; Lam. iii. 13.

[5] Jer. xii. 2: cf. Pss. vii. 10 (EVV. 9), xxvi. 2; Jer. xi. 20, xvii. 10, xx. 12, all of Yahweh's power to scrutinize the heart and the reins; also Ps. xvi. 7.

Possibly the liver (כָּבֵד) should also be included in the above list; for in Lam. ii. 11 it is apparently said to be 'poured out' in grief. Such at least is the reading of M.T., whereas LXX, L, and S read כְּבֵדִי, 'my glory'. Some scholars would read כָּבֵד for כָּבוֹד, which is the reading of M.T., in such passages as Gen. xlix. 6; Pss. vii. 6 (EVV. 5), xvi. 9, xxx. 13 (EVV. 12), lvii. 9 (EVV. 8), cviii. 2 (EVV. 1). Cf., for example, Gunkel, H.K. (1926), on Ps. vii. 6; A. Bertholet, op. cit., pp. 12 f.; Eichrodt, op. cit., ii, p. 74, ii–iii, 4th edit., p. 96; also (in part) H. W. Robinson, e.g. in *The Christian Doctrine of Man*, p. 23. The fact that psychical activity is manifested by other parts of the body, coupled with the existence of Accadian parallels, undoubtedly lends support to this suggestion. Nevertheless it must be received with caution. In J, with its strongly anthropomorphic conception of Yahweh, the term כָּבוֹד is quite clearly used to denote the radiant person of the Godhead (Exod. xxxiii. 17–23); and in P this is used in a way which shows that the conception of His 'Glory', like that of the 'Name', for example, is well on the way towards taking its place amongst the so-called 'Hypostases' of later Jewish thought, e.g. in Exod. xvi. 10, xxiv. 16 f., xxix. 43, and so often. Cf. *The Cultic Prophet in Ancient Israel*, p. 36, n. 1, 2nd edit., p. 38, n. 6, and the authorities there cited. Accordingly it may well be that the term was used in much the same way to denote the person of man in all its dignity and worth; and its use with a suffix as a sort of glorified personal pronoun is a simple but obvious development from this. Cf. its continued use in modern Hebrew, e.g. הַשֵׁיךְ בִּכְבוֹדוֹ וּבְעַצְמוֹ, i.e. 'the sheikh himself' or 'the sheikh in person'; and see further W. Caspari, *Die Bedeutungen der Wortsippe* כבד *im Hebräischen* (1908), pp. 26, 133 f.; Pedersen, *Israel I–II*, pp. 176 ff., 408 (i.e. p. 185, n. 1), E.T., pp. 228 ff., 519 (i.e. p. 239, n. 1); and G. von Rad, in *Th.W.N.T.* ii (1935), pp. 240–5, esp. p. 241. The fact is that each passage must be examined on its merits: cf. now G. R. Driver, in *J.R.A.S.* (1948), p. 175, n. 2.

[6] There seems to be no essential difference between the two terms לֵב and לֵבָב; and if M.T. may be trusted, these occur at least 850 times

importance was, of course, unknown; for the Israelites, in common with the other peoples of the ancient world, appear to have learnt nothing of the circulation of the blood. Nevertheless, just as the foregoing illustrations make it clear that, even if they knew nothing of the nervous system as such, they were well aware of its presence and operation, so the central importance of the heart was obvious enough; and as a result we find it taking the place of the brain in their thinking as the focal point of a whole range of psychical activity. Thus at the purely emotional level it is quite often represented on the one hand as the seat of cheerfulness, gladness, or joy,[1] and on the other as affected with grief, despondency, vexation, or distress.[2] Indeed, at this level, while associated occasionally with anger[3] and even hatred[4] or jealousy,[5] it appears as specially subject to fear, and in this condition may be said to tremble, melt, show signs of weakness, or even lose all signs of life.[6] On the other hand

(including 1 Kings xii. 33 (Q)). Cf. now F. H. von Meyenfeldt, *Het hart (leb, lebab) in het Oude Testament* (1950), p. 222. The supposedly feminine form in Ezek. xvi. 30 apparently corresponds to the Accadian LIBBĀTU (pl.), 'wrath': cf. G. R. Driver, in *J.T.S.* xxix (1928), p. 393, and xxxii (1931), p. 366, and see now K.B., s.v.

[1] i.e. 53 clear examples of the type: (a) Judges xviii. 20; Ruth iii. 7: (b) Prov. xv. 13: (c) 1 Sam. ii. 1; Pss. xiii. 6 (EVV. 5), xxviii. 7, lxxxiv. 3 (EVV. 2); Isa. lxvi. 14.

[2] i.e. 41 clear examples (including those which, like Gen. vi. 6 (J), refer to God), the various types being represented by: (a) 1 Sam. i. 8; Ps. xiii. 3 (EVV. 2); Prov. xiv. 10, 13, xv. 13; Isa. lxv. 14; Jer. viii. 18; Lam. i. 20: (b) Pss. lxi. 3 (EVV. 2), cix. 16, cxliii. 4; Prov. xiii. 12; Eccles. ii. 20: (c) Ps. lxxiii. 21; Eccles. xi. 10: (d) Pss. xxv. 17, lv. 5 (EVV. 4), cii. 5 (EVV. 4); Prov. xii. 25; Isa. xv. 5; Jer. iv. 19, xx. 9, xxiii. 9. Cf. (of freedom from distress) Ps. cxix. 32; Isa. lx. 5.

[3] Deut. xix. 6; 2 Kings vi. 11; Job xv. 12; Prov. xix. 3: cf. Ps. xxxix. 4 (EVV. 3).   [4] Lev. xix. 17 (H).   [5] Prov. xxiii. 17.

[6] i.e. at least 46 examples, the outstanding types being best illustrated by: (a) Deut. xxviii. 67: (b) Ps. xxvii. 3: (c) Deut. xxviii. 65; 1 Sam. iv. 13 or Job xxxvii. 1; Isa. vii. 2: (d) Joshua vii. 5 or Ps. xxii. 15 (EVV. 14) and so at least 12 times in all; Ezek. xxi. 20 (EVV. 15), but see P. Joüon, in *Biblica*, vii (1926), pp. 165 ff.: (e) Deut. xx. 3, and similarly 9 times in all: (f) Gen. xlv. 26 (E); 1 Sam. xxv. 37. The following (occasionally typical) passages are also deserving of notice: Gen. xlii. 28 (J) and Ps. xl. 13 (EVV. 12), both of 'losing heart', as we should say; 1 Sam. xvii. 32, of a 'sinking' heart; Ps. xxxviii. 11 (EVV. 10); Isa. xxi. 4, xxxv. 4 (cf. xxxii. 4); Jer. xlix. 22; Ezek. xiv. 5.

and at the other extreme, however, the heart may also be
referred to as firm or strong, and therefore as the seat of
boldness or courage;[1] and it is idiomatic as well as axiomatic that to speak to the heart in a certain way is to offer
reassurance or encouragement.[2]

However, for all that the heart is thus brought so often
into relation with man's psychical life at the emotional
level (and the extent of its use in this connexion is not always
accorded its due weight), it is as the seat or instrument of
his intellectual and volitional activity that it figures most
prominently in Israelite thinking. Thus the term for 'heart',
besides being used with a force which approximates to what
we should call 'mind'[3] or 'intellect',[4] is frequently employed
by metonymy to denote one's thought and therefore, on
occasion, one's wish, purpose, or resolve;[5] for one's thought

[1] Pss. xxvii. 14, xxxi. 25 (EVV. 24); Amos ii. 16. In these passages, of
course, the force of √אמץ is different from that in Deut. ii. 30, xv. 7;
2 Chron. xxxvi. 13 (as noted below, p. 80, n. 4). Cf., too, 2 Sam. vii. 27 (i.e. of
'taking heart', as we say, and therefore the opposite of Gen. xlii. 28 (J), &c.),
xvii. 10; Ezek. xxii. 14; Dan. xi. 25. In Song of Sol. iv. 9 the verb denominative *Pi'ēl* may have the meaning 'to hearten', and so be included here (cf.
R.V. mgn.); but unfortunately it is somewhat ambiguous, as it is conceivable
that it means 'to enchant', i.e. as stealing one's heart away (cf. EVV., R.S.V.)!
See, for example, A. Harper, C.B. (1902), *in loc.*

[2] i.e. in the familiar idiom which is paraphrased in the English Versions
by 'to speak comfortably (friendly, kindly) to' someone: Gen. xxxiv. 3, l.
21 (both JE); Judges xix. 3; Ruth ii. 13; 2 Sam. xix. 8 (EVV. 7); 2 Chron.
xxx. 22, xxxii. 6; Isa. xl. 2; Hos. ii. 16 (EVV. 14). Cf. now R.S.V. on 2 Chron.
xxx. 22, xxxii. 6.

[3] Cf., in addition to the many examples cited in the following notes, Deut.
xv. 9, xxx. 14; Judges v. 15, 16; 2 Sam. vi. 16 (= 1 Chron. xv. 29); 1 Kings
iii. 9; 2 Kings v. 26; Neh. v. 7; Job xvii. 11; Pss. xxvii. 8, xxxvi. 2 (EVV. 1),
xl. 11 (EVV. 10), xli. 7 (EVV. 6), xliv. 22 (EVV. 21), xlv. 2 (EVV. 1), lxvi.
18, lxxiii. 7, lxxvii. 7 (EVV. 6), lxxviii. 18, lxxxiii. 6 (EVV. 5), lxxxiv. 6
(EVV. 5); Prov. iv. 4, 21, vi. 14, vii. 10, xvi. 1, xx. 5, xxiii. 33, xxvii. 19;
Eccles. ii. 3, iii. 11, v. 1 (EVV. 2), vii. 26; Song of Sol. v. 2; Isa. x. 7, xxxii.
6, li. 7; Jer. xxiii. 26; Lam. iii. 41; Hos. vii. 6 (?): also (of God) Job x. 13,
xxxvi. 5 (?); Isa. lxiii. 4; Jer. xxiii. 20, xxx. 24.

[4] Job viii. 10, xii. 3, xxxiv. 10, 34; Prov. xv. 32. Cf. the force of the verb
denominative *Niph'al* in Job xi. 12.

[5] Cf. Judges xvi. 15 (i.e. of sharing one's thoughts), 17, 18; 1 Kings viii.
39 (= 2 Chron. vi. 30); Pss. xx. 5 (EVV. 4), lv. 22 (EVV. 21), lxii. 9 (EVV. 8),
lxiv. 7 (EVV. 6), cxxxix. 23; Prov. x. 20, xxv. 3, xxviii. 26; Lam. ii. 19;
Dan. xi. 27, 28: also (of God) 1 Sam. xiii. 14; 2 Sam. vii. 21; 1 Kings ix. 3

or wish is essentially 'that which is in the heart', or, as we should say, 'what one has in mind'.[1] Similarly, whereas we speak of a matter in English as 'entering one's mind', the Israelite says that it 'mounts upon the heart';[2] and in much the same way 'to lay to heart' is 'to bear in mind',[3] 'to bring back to the heart' is 'to recall to mind',[4] and for a thing to 'turn aside' from the heart is for one to 'forget' it.[5] Further, 'to say *in* the heart'[6] (or, much less frequently, 'to say *to* one's heart', i.e. in English idiom 'to say to oneself')[7] is the simple, normal way of saying 'to think'; and this corresponds to the comparatively frequent association of the heart with √חשׁב, 'to think' or (in its implication of thinking ahead) 'to plan'.[8] Similarly, 'to apply the heart' to a matter is 'to pay attention' to it or even occasionally 'to concentrate' upon it.[9] Accordingly 'wisdom'

(= 2 Chron. vii. 16); Jer. iii. 15. For corresponding examples of such metonymy, see above, p. 49, n. 4.

[1] Cf. (*a*) Deut. viii. 2; 1 Sam. ix. 19, xiv. 7; 2 Sam. vii. 3 (= 1 Chron. xvii. 2); 2 Chron. xxxii. 31; also (of God) 1 Sam. ii. 35; 2 Kings x. 30: (*b*) Joshua xiv. 7; 1 Kings x. 2 (= 2 Chron. ix. 1); similarly 1 Kings viii. 17 f. (= 2 Chron. vi. 7 f.); 1 Chron. xxii. 7, xxviii. 2; 2 Chron. i. 11, xxiv. 4, xxix. 10.

[2] 2 Kings xii. 5 (EVV. 4); Isa. lxv. 17; Jer. iii. 16, li. 50; Ezek. xiv. 3, 4, 7, xxxviii. 10: and (of God) Jer. vii. 31, xix. 5, xxxii. 35, xliv. 21. See also 2 Chron. vii. 11 (as compared with 1 Kings ix. 1).

[3] (*a*) Deut. xi. 18; Isa. xlii. 25, xlvii. 7, lvii. 1, 11; Jer. xii. 11; Dan. i. 8; Mal. ii. 2: (*b*) 2 Sam. xiii. 33, xix. 20 (EVV. 19): (*c*) 1 Sam. xxi. 13 (EVV. 12); Job xxii. 22: (*d*) Eccles. vii. 2, ix. 1 (as distinct from Neh. ii. 12, vii. 5: cf. Ezra vii. 27; Ezek. iii. 10). Cf. Deut. vi. 6; Pss. xxxvii. 31, cxix. 11; Prov. vi. 21: also the simile of Prov. iii. 3, vii. 3; Jer. xvii. 1, xxxi. 33.

[4] Deut. iv. 39, xxx. 1; 1 Kings viii. 47 (= 2 Chron. vi. 37); Isa. xliv. 19, xlvi. 8; Lam. iii. 21.

[5] Deut. iv. 9: cf. Ps. xxxi. 13 (EVV. 12).

[6] Gen. xxvii. 41 (J); Deut. ix. 4; Esther vi. 6; Ps. xiv. 1 (= liii. 2 (EVV. 1)); Eccles. ii. 15a; Isa. xlvii. 8, 10; Jer. v. 24; Zeph. i. 12, &c. (30 times in all): similarly (*a*) Ps. xv. 2; Eccles. ii. 15b: (*b*) Deut. xxix. 18 (EVV. 19); Job i. 5.

[7] (*a*) 1 Sam. xxvii. 1; and (of God) Gen. viii. 21 (J): (*b*) Gen. xxiv. 45 (J); 1 Sam. i. 13; Hos. vii. 2: cf. Eccles. i. 16.

[8] Gen. vi. 5 (cf. viii. 21 (both J)); 1 Chron. xxix. 18; Ps. cxl. 3 (EVV. 2); Prov. vi. 18, xvi. 9, xix. 21; Isa. x. 7; Zech. vii. 10, viii. 17: also (of God) Ps. xxxiii. 11. Cf. Pss. xix. 15 (EVV. 14), xlix. 4 (EVV. 3); Prov. xv. 28, xxiv. 2; Isa. xxxiii. 18, lix. 13.

[9] (*a*) Exod. ix. 21 (J); Deut. xxxii. 46; 1 Sam. ix. 20, xxv. 25; 2 Sam. xviii. 3; Ezek. xl. 4, xliv. 5; Hag. i. 5, 7, ii. 15, 18; also (of heavenly beings or God)

(חכם√)[1] and 'understanding' (בין√),[2] as well as 'knowledge' (ידע√),[3] all of which are normally esteemed for their practical value, are frequently brought into association with the heart, as when God is said to have given Solomon 'wisdom and understanding and breadth of heart like the sand which is on the sea-shore';[4] and this in turn corresponds to the fact that to be 'lacking' in heart or, as we might say, 'lacking in intelligence' (חֲסַר־לֵב) is to be stupid or foolish in one's behaviour.[5]

The heart with its latent desire[6] is thus recognized as a governing factor in one's behaviour; so that to do a thing 'from one's heart' is to act spontaneously or on one's own initiative, i.e. 'of oneself'.[7] Hence it is through the instrumentality of the heart that a man decides upon one particular course of action as against another; and such choice of direction may be regarded as due either to this spontaneous action within the heart or to the influencing of the heart by external forces, human or divine.[8] Accordingly, if anyone

Job i. 8, ii. 3, xxxiv. 14 (?); Isa. xli. 22: (*b*) Exod. vii. 23 (J); 1 Sam. iv. 20; 2 Sam. xiii. 20; Pss. xlviii. 14 (EVV. 13), lxii. 11 (EVV. 10); Prov. xxii. 17, xxiv. 32, xxvii. 23; Jer. xxxi. 21; also (of God) Job vii. 17: (*c*) 2 Chron. xi. 16; Prov. xxiii. 26; Eccles. i. 13, 17, vii. 21, viii. 9, 16; Dan. x. 12: (*d*) Prov. xxiii. 12.

[1] Exod. xxviii. 3, xxxi. 6, xxxv. 10, 25, 26, 34 f., xxxvi. 1, 2, 8 (all P); 1 Kings iii. 12, x. 24 (= 2 Chron. ix. 23); Job xxxvii. 24; Ps. xc. 12; Prov. ii. 10, x. 8, xi. 29, xiv. 33, xvi. 21, 23, xvii. 16, xxiii. 15; Eccles. i. 16 f., ii. 3, vii. 4, viii. 5, x. 2: also (of God) Job ix. 4.

[2] 1 Kings iii. 12; Prov. ii. 2, viii. 5 (but note LXX), xiv. 33, xv. 14, xvi. 21, xviii. 15, xix. 8; Isa. vi. 10, xxxii. 4. Cf. Job xvii. 4; Isa. xliv. 18.

[3] Deut. viii. 5, xxix. 3; Joshua xxiii. 14; 1 Kings ii. 44; Prov. xiv. 10, xv. 14, xviii. 15, xxii. 17; Eccles. i. 16 f., vii. 22, 25, viii. 5, 16; Isa. xxxii. 4; Jer. xxiv. 7.

[4] 1 Kings v. 9 (EVV. iv. 29).

[5] Cf. Prov. vi. 32, vii. 7, ix. 4, 16, x. 13, 21, xi. 12, xii. 11, xv. 21, xvii. 18, xxiv. 30; similarly Eccles. x. 3. Cf. (*a*) Prov. xvii. 16; Jer. v. 21; Hos. vii. 11; also Job xii. 24; Hos. iv. 11: (*b*) with specific reference to stupidity or folly, Prov. xii. 23, xv. 7, xviii. 2, xxii. 15; Eccles. vii. 4, x. 2.

[6] Cf. Pss. xxi. 3 (EVV. 2), xxxvii. 4; Prov. vi. 25; Eccles. ii. 22.

[7] Cf. Num. xvi. 28 (J), xxiv. 13 (J); 1 Kings xii. 33 (Q); Neh. vi. 8; Ezek. xiii. 2, 17 (cf. Jer. xxiii. 16): also (of God) Lam. iii. 33.

[8] The most picturesque idiom in this connexion is that which refers literally to the 'stealing' of a man's heart (i.e. with the obvious intention of leading him astray), as in Gen. xxxi. 20, 26 (both E); 2 Sam. xv. 6 (cf. verse 13): but

80 *The Vitality of the Individual*

persists in following a certain course against another's advice, this may be regarded as a mark of stubbornness,[1] and in such a case it is idiomatic to speak of the heart as being (or as being made) 'heavy',[2] 'hard',[3] or 'strong';[4] but where agreement exists there is clear evidence of 'one heart' or, as we should say, 'unanimity'.[5]

All in all, therefore, it is only to be expected that the employment of synecdoche should also take place in respect of the heart; and this is frequently the case, as when the Israelite sage thus bids his pupil not to exult over the misfortunes of his opponents:[6]

> Be not glad at the downfall of thine enemy,
> Nor let thy heart rejoice when he stumbleth.

see in general (a) Job xxxi. 7; Ezek. xi. 21, xx. 16, xxxiii. 31: (b) Exod. xiv. 5 (J); Ps. cv. 25: (c) Exod. xxv. 2, xxxv. 5, 22, 29 (all P); 2 Chron. xxix. 31: (d) Num. xxxii. 7, 9 (JEP): (e) Exod. xxxv. 21 (cf. verse 26), xxxvi. 2 (all P): (f) Joshua xxiv. 23 (E); Judges ix. 3; 2 Sam. xix. 15 (EVV. 14); 1 Kings viii. 58, xi. 2, 3, 4, 9; Pss. cxix. 36, 112, cxli. 4; Prov. xxi. 1; Isa. xliv. 20: (g) 1 Kings xviii. 37; Ezra vi. 22: (h) Ps. xliv. 19 (EVV. 18); Prov. xiv. 14: (i) Deut. xvii. 17; Jer. xvii. 5; Ezek. vi. 9:(j) Deut. xxix. 17 (EVV. 18), xxx. 17: (k) Deut. xi. 16; Job xxxi. 9, 27: (l) 1 Kings xii. 27; Mal. iii. 24 (EVV. iv. 6): cf. Isa. lvii. 17: (m) the following sporadic passages, Num. xv. 39 (P); Deut. v. 26 (EVV. 29); 1 Sam. x. 26; Neh. iii. 38 (EVV. iv. 6); Pss. lviii. 3 (EVV. 2), xcv. 10; Prov. v. 12, vii. 25, xxiii. 19; Eccles. vii. 7, xi. 9; Jer. xxii. 17; Ezek. iii. 10. Note, too, the indication of conflicting thought (or what we should call one's conscience) in 1 Sam. xxiv. 6 (EVV. 5), xxv. 31; 2 Sam. xxiv. 10; Job xxvii. 6: also the stunning effect of disaster as described in Deut. xxviii. 28; Jer. iv. 9.

[1] Deut. xxix. 18 (EVV. 19); Ps. lxxxi. 13 (EVV. 12); Jer. iii. 17, vii. 24, ix. 13, xi. 8, xiii. 10, xvi. 12, xviii. 12, xxiii. 17: cf. Jer. v. 23.

[2] Exod. vii. 14, viii. 11 (EVV. 15), 28 (EVV. 32), ix. 7, 34, x. 1 (all J); 1 Sam. vi. 6.

[3] Exod. vii. 3 (P); Ps. xcv. 8; Prov. xxviii. 14: also Isa. lxiii. 17.

[4] (a) Exod. iv. 21 (E), vii. 13, 22, viii. 15 (EVV. 19), ix. 12 (all P), 35 (E), x. 20, 27 (both E), xi. 10, xiv. 4, 8, 17 (all P); Joshua xi. 20; Ezek. ii. 4: (b) Deut. ii. 30, xv. 7; 2 Chron. xxxvi. 13 (cf. p. 77, n. 1). Cf., perhaps, Ps. lxxvi. 6 (EVV. 5); Isa. xlvi. 12.

[5] 1 Chron. xii. 39 (EVV. 38); 2 Chron. xxx. 12; Jer. xxxii. 39; Ezek. xi. 19. In the last two passages LXX has the rendering 'another heart', and S, 'a new heart'; but M.T. represents the more likely reading in at least the former instance (vide comm.). Cf. (a) 1 Chron. xii. 18 (EVV. 17); Ps. lxxxvi. 11 (i.e. following the vocalization of M.T. rather than that of LXX and S): (b) 2 Sam. xix. 15 (EVV. 14); 2 Kings x. 15: also (c) the idiom for discord or duplicity (לֵב וָלֵב) in 1 Chron. xii. 34 (EVV. 33); Ps. xii. 3 (EVV. 2).

[6] Prov. xxiv. 17.

Similarly, he may exhort his pupil to bear such an injunction in mind by saying:[1]

> My son, forget not my teaching,
> But let thy heart keep my commandments.

As a final and even better illustration, however, we may take the language of Isaiah, when he contrasts the plans of the Assyrian invader with those of Yahweh, i.e.:[2]

> But it is not thus that *he* planneth,
> And 'tis not thus that *his heart* doth devise.

The parallelism in all these cases (as in some of the many others which are available) should be noted carefully; for it brings out quite clearly the presence of synecdoche with its implied grasping of a totality.[3] In the last passage, for example, the Hebrew might almost be rendered:

> But it is not thus that *he* planneth,
> And 'tis not thus that *he himself* doth devise.[4]

Indeed, in the case of the heart the employment of synecdoche is the more ready and the more common because the heart in all its wide range of emotional, intellectual, and volitional activity is obviously found to be of supreme importance to the *ego* or unit of consciousness (אֲנִי or אָנֹכִי) as an organ of self-expression.[5] Moreover, it is to

---

[1] Prov. iii. 1.   [2] x. 7.

[3] The following are a few selected examples, which have been chosen for the most part because of the parallelism or some other equally instructive feature in the wording of the context: Lev. xxvi. 41 (H); Deut. xi. 16, xvii. 17, xx. 3, xxx. 17; 1 Sam. i. 8; 1 Kings ii. 44; Neh. v. 7; Job xv. 12, xxxi. 9, 27; Pss. xxv. 17, xxvii. 8, xxviii. 7, xli. 7 (EVV. 6), xliv. 19 (EVV. 18), xlv. 2 (EVV. 1), lxxiii. 21, lxxxiv. 3 (EVV. 2), as quoted above, p. 38, cxii. 7; Prov. iv. 4, v. 12, vi. 18, vii. 25, xv. 14, xx. 9, xxiii. 33, xxxi. 11; Eccles. v. 1 (EVV. 2), vii. 25 (?), viii. 5; Isa. vi. 10, vii. 4, xxxii. 4, 6, xliv. 20; Jer. xvii. 5, li. 46; Ezek. vi. 9, xx. 16. See also the interesting construction in 1 Chron. xxii. 7, xxviii. 2.

[4] Cf. the analogous reflexive force in Gen. xviii. 5 (J); Judges xix. 5, 8.

[5] In the above discussion of the various parts of the body considerable stress has been laid upon the employment of synecdoche, because it is the failure to give this its due weight which has led to the theory that the various organs and limbs of the body are to be regarded as functioning independently or as being 'self-operative' and, therefore, as pointing to a belief in what has been called 'a diffusion of consciousness'. Cf. H. W. Robinson, *The Christian*

be observed that, as such, it is ultimately regarded as specially subject to the influence of the רוּחַ, for the reader must already have been struck by the many close parallels between the references to the רוּחַ and those to the heart, and these parallels should be borne constantly in mind from now on.

For the religious teachers of Israel, however, there is an ideal standard of behaviour by which one's life should be governed;[1] and in view of the important role ascribed to the

Doctrine of Man, pp. 22 ff.; 'Hebrew Psychology', in *The People and the Book*, pp. 362 ff.; *Inspiration and Revelation in the Old Testament*, pp. 71 ff.: L. H. Brockington, in *J.T.S.* xlvii (1946), pp. 1 ff. In the present writer's opinion this is quite without justification, being based upon too literal a reading of the text. After all, we should not dream of taking the Israelite literally when he speaks of his heart as melting with fear, and especially when the psalmist describes his heart as melted in the midst of his bowels (Ps. xxii. 15 (EVV. 14): cf. p. 76, n. 6 (*d*))! This being the case, it is difficult to see why one should be forced to accept his words at their face value, when he speaks of the flesh as longing, the palate as discerning, the eye as bearing witness, and so on. (Cf. Robinson, op. cit., p. 72.) Again, to take another simple illustration, the normal Hebrew idiom for paying attention is of the type 'Incline thine ear'—not 'O ear, incline thyself', as one would expect if the various organs and limbs of the body were really regarded as being 'self-operative'! See Ps. xlv. 11 (EVV. 10); Prov. iv. 20, v. 1; and so often. Cf., too, Prov. xxiii. 12; also Ps. x. 17 and Prov. ii. 2 (vide G.K., § 144*lm*, as cited above, p. 64, n. 1): in contrast to the much rarer and mostly late expressions in (*a*) Isa. xxxii. 3: (*b*) Neh. i. 6, 11: (*c*) 2 Chron. vi. 40, vii. 15; Ps. cxxx. 2, all of which may be explained as simple examples of synecdoche. What is more, to say in consequence that 'the Hebrews only gradually reached a conception of the independence and unity of the individual, even as they emerged bit by bit from the more primitive ways of thought' (Brockington, op. cit., p. 3) is to overlook the existence from the first of the personal pronouns in the rich variety of their independent, prefixed, affixed, and suffixed forms. (P. van Imschoot, *Théologie de l'Ancien Testament*, ii (1956), p. 36, n. 1, appears to think that synecdoche of the type under discussion is a survival from a more rudimentary stage when such independent activity could indeed be attributed to certain parts of the body, and that it may be doubted if the Hebrew writers had advanced beyond this level of thought; but, apart from the fact that van Imschoot fails to meet the foregoing objections, it should be borne in mind that, even if such synecdoche could be shown to reflect a more rudimentary level, one would need to beware of inferring too readily that such forms of speech still preserved their original associations. Cf., for example, the words of caution offered by H. Graf Reventlow, ' "Sein Blut komme über sein Haupt" ', *V.T.* xi (1960), pp. 311–27.)

[1] A fuller discussion of the relevant terminology (with special reference to √צדק) is reserved for the immediate sequel to this monograph, i.e. a similar study to be entitled *The Vitality of Society in the Thought of Ancient Israel*.

heart as an organ of self-expression it is not surprising that,
like some of the other parts of the body which we have
noticed, it should be found with ethical associations, and
that conformity with this ideal should sometimes be described in terms of the 'purity' (e.g. ברר√),[1] 'integrity'
(תמם√),[2] or 'straightforwardness' (ישר√)[3] of the heart. In
the last resort, however, such conformity with the ideal is
a conformity with what we should call the will of Yahweh,
who is its author and guardian; so that such 'integrity' is
reached only as one learns to respond to Yahweh 'with *all*
one's heart'.[4] Where such unwavering allegiance occurs, it

---

[1] Pss. xxiv. 4, lxxiii. 1. Cf. (זכה√) Ps. lxxiii. 13; Prov. xx. 9: and (טהר√)
Ps. li. 12 (EVV. 10), as quoted below, p. 86; Prov. xxii. 11; also the parallelism
of Prov. xx. 9. Observe in particular the reference to one's being not only
'pure in heart' but also 'clean of hands' (i.e., as we should say, 'innocent in
thought and deed') in Pss. xxiv. 4, lxxiii. 13.

[2] Gen. xx. 5, 6 (E); 1 Kings ix. 4; Pss. lxxviii. 72, ci. 2, cxix. 80. Observe
here, too, the additional reference to the part played by the hands as well as
the heart (i.e. as summing up one's behaviour 'in thought and deed') in
Gen. xx. 5 (E); Ps. lxxviii. 72.

[3] Deut. ix. 5; 1 Kings iii. 6 (cf. ix. 4, xiv. 8); 1 Chron. xxix. 17; 2 Chron.
xxix. 34; Job xxxiii. 3 (?); Pss. vii. 11 (EVV. 10), xi. 2, xxxii. 11, xxxvi. 11
(EVV. 10), lxiv. 11 (EVV. 10), xciv. 15, xcvii. 11, cxix. 7, cxxv. 4. The text
of Job xxxiii. 3 is a matter of dispute (cf., for example, Driver–Gray and
Dhorme, *in loc.*); but it is not to be rejected too readily, for it yields sense as
it stands. Note also the language employed by Jehu when he asks Jehonadab
if he is in agreement with his policy, 2 Kings x. 15: cf. S, rather than LXX
which is commonly followed, e.g. by C. F. Burney, *Notes on the Hebrew Text
of the Books of Kings* (1903), *in loc.*; and see now, for an attempt to defend
the vocalization of M.T., J. A. Montgomery and H. S. Gehman, I.C.C.
(1951), *in loc.* Observe, too, that ישר√ may imply, not only that one is
'straightforward', but also that one is, as we say, 'on the level'!

[4] Cf. 1 Sam. vii. 3, xii. 20, 24; 1 Kings viii. 23 (= 2 Chron. vi. 14), xiv.
8; 2 Kings x. 31; 2 Chron. xv. 15, xxii. 9, xxxi. 21; Pss. ix. 2 (EVV. 1),
lxxxvi. 12, cxi. 1, cxix. 2, 10, 34, 58, 69, 145, cxxxviii. 1; Prov. iii. 5; Jer.
iii. 10, xxiv. 7, xxix. 13; Joel ii. 12. As the heart is so frequently associated
with intellectual and volitional activities, this expression is often reinforced
by adding 'and with all one's נֶפֶשׁ', a term which tends to be employed, as
we have seen, with a more emotional content. Cf. Deut. iv. 29, x. 12, xi. 13,
xiii. 4 (EVV. 3), xxvi. 16, xxx. 2, 6, 10; Joshua xxii. 5; 1 Kings ii. 4, viii. 48
(= 2 Chron. vi. 38); 2 Kings xxiii. 3 (= 2 Chron. xxxiv. 31); 2 Chron. xv. 12:
also 1 Chron. xxii. 19, xxviii. 9. Indeed, on two occasions this characteristic-
ally Deuteronomic expression is reinforced yet again by adding 'and with all
one's might (מְאֹד)': i.e. Deut. vi. 5; 2 Kings xxiii. 25. Finally, note the slightly
different association of the heart with the term נֶפֶשׁ in Joshua xxiii. 14;
1 Chron. xxviii. 9: and (of God) 1 Sam. ii. 35; Jer. xxxii. 41.

denotes 'a faithful heart' (לֵבָב נֶאֱמָן)[1] or, as it is more often expressed, 'a steadfast heart' (לֵב נָכוֹן),[2] which thus corresponds to the ideal of 'a steadfast רוּחַ' (רוּחַ נָכוֹן);[3] and the heart may then be described as being 'at one' (שָׁלֵם) with Yahweh.[4]

Accordingly Yahweh is primarily concerned, not with a man's outward appearance, but with his heart; for obviously it is here that a man's real character finds its most ready expression.[5] Indeed, it is axiomatic for Israel's religious teachers that man is constantly subject to Yahweh's scrutiny; and this is expressed in clearly idiomatic fashion by saying that He 'examines' (usually בחן√) men's hearts[6] or (if one would emphasize His power to know a man through and through) that He examines 'the reins and the heart',[7] as one tests silver and gold.[8] In other words, Yahweh is so concerned with man's behaviour that He is regularly occupied in 'pondering' (תכן√) every individual heart or, what amounts to the same thing, every רוּחַ.[9] In fact it is He alone who knows the heart of man for what it really is;[10] and He knows that on the whole it tends to be, not 'straightforward' or, possibly, 'on the level' (ישׁר√),[11]

---

[1] Vide Neh. ix. 8. Cf. (*a*) 1 Sam. xii. 24; 1 Kings ii. 4: (*b*) Pss. xxviii. 7, cxii. 7: also (*c*) Ps. lxxiii. 26.

[2] Vide Pss. lvii. 8 (EVV. 7) = cviii. 2 (EVV. 1), lxxviii. 37, cxii. 7 (cf. verse 8). Cf. the corresponding use of the *Hiph'il* in 1 Sam. vii. 3; 1 Chron. xxix. 18; 2 Chron. xii. 14, xix. 3, xx. 33, xxx. 19; Ezra vii. 10; Job xi. 13; Pss. x. 17, lxxviii. 8. There is a close parallel, of course, in the Accadian KŪN LIBBI ('steadfastness of heart') and LIBBU KĒNU ('a steadfast heart').

[3] Ps. li. 12 (EVV. 10), as quoted above, p. 36, and below, p. 86: cf. the parallelism of Ps. lxxviii. 8.

[4] 1 Kings viii. 61, xi. 4, xv. 3, 14 (cf. 2 Chron. xv. 17). See also (*a*) 2 Chron. xvi. 9: (*b*) 2 Kings xx. 3 (= Isa. xxxviii. 3); 1 Chron. xxviii. 9, xxix. 9, 19; 2 Chron. xix. 9, xxv. 2. Cf., too, 1 Chron. xii. 39 (EVV. 38), as cited above, p. 80, n. 5.

[5] 1 Sam. xvi. 7.

[6] 1 Chron. xxix. 17; Ps. xvii. 3; Prov. xvii. 3; Jer. xii. 3. Cf. 1 Chron. xxviii. 9; 2 Chron. xxxii. 31; Pss. xliv. 22 (EVV. 21), cxxxix. 23.

[7] Cf. Pss. vii. 10 (EVV. 9), xxvi. 2; Jer. xi. 20, xvii. 10, xx. 12.

[8] Prov. xvii. 3.   [9] Cf. Prov. xvi. 2, xxi. 2, xxiv. 12.

[10] See 1 Kings viii. 39 (= 2 Chron. vi. 30): also Ps. xxxiii. 15 (cf. xciv. 9); Prov. xv. 11.

[11] See above, p. 83, n. 3.

but 'crooked' or 'pervert' (עקשׁ√),[1] because more often than not the shape of its thought or, as we might say, man's frame of mind (i.e. יֵצֶר (מַחְשָׁבֹת) לֵב הָאָדָם) does not conform to His ideal standard but is bent on evil (רעע√).[2] What is more, this failure to fulfil one's moral obligations is associated time and again with what are obviously regarded as two major defects on the part of the heart, i.e. a proneness to deceit[3] and, above all, a tendency to be lofty or swollen with pride.[4]

Finally, it is to be observed that this failure to act fittingly or aright in response to Yahweh's demands is ascribed, on the one hand, to the 'fatty' condition of the heart[5] or (somewhat similarly) to its need for 'circumcision',[6]

---

[1] Ps. ci. 4; Prov. xi. 20, xvii. 20: cf. (עוה√) Prov. xii. 8.

[2] Cf. (in addition to such indirect association of רעע√ with the heart as occurs in Deut. xv. 9; Ps. ci. 4) Gen. vi. 5 (J), viii. 21 (J); 1 Sam. xvii. 28; 1 Kings ii. 44; Pss. xxviii. 3, cxl. 3 (EVV. 2), cxli. 4; Prov. vi. 14, xii. 20, xxvi. 23; Eccles. viii. 11, ix. 3; Jer. iii. 17, iv. 14, vii. 24, ix. 13 (LXX, S), xi. 8, xvi. 12, xviii. 12; Dan. xi. 27: similarly Isa. xxxii. 6. See also (apropos the use of the term יֵצֶר in Gen. vi. 5, viii. 21) Deut. xxxi. 21; 1 Chron. xxviii. 9, xxix. 18; Isa. xxvi. 3; and bear in mind the rabbinic development of this conception in terms of the so-called 'good impulse' (יצר טוב) and 'bad impulse' (יצר הרע). Cf., for example, W. Bousset, *Die Religion des Judentums im späthellenistischen Zeitalter*, 3rd edit. rev. by H. Gressmann (1926), pp. 402 ff.; and especially G. F. Moore, *Judaism in the First Centuries of the Christian Era: The Age of the Tannaim*, i (1927), pp. 479 ff. See also Job xxxvi. 13 (cf. Isa. xxxii. 6), i.e. the associated use of the term חָנֵף, which (in comparison with the corresponding Arabic term حَنِيفٌ, as used, for example, to denote the pious Muslim) offers yet another example of semantic polarization, i.e. a 'bent' in the wrong direction! Cf. حَنَفَ, 'to lean, incline'; and see above, p. 22, n. 3.

[3] Pss. xii. 3 (EVV. 2), xxviii. 3; Prov. xii. 20, xxiii. 7, xxvi. 25; Isa. xxix. 13; Jer. xiv. 14, xvii. 9, xxiii. 26; Hos. x. 2: cf. Lam. iii. 41; Joel ii. 13.

[4] Cf. (a) 2 Chron. xxvi. 16, xxxii. 25, 26; Ps. cxxxi. 1; Prov. xvi. 5, xviii. 12; Ezek. xxviii. 2, 5 f., 17 (as against 2 Chron. xvii. 6, where this expression is used in a good sense): (b) Isa. ix. 8, x. 12; Dan. viii. 25: (c) 1 Sam. xvii. 28; Jer. xlix. 16 (= Obad. 3): (d) 2 Kings xiv. 10 (= 2 Chron. xxv. 19): (e) Deut. viii. 14, xvii. 20; Jer. xlviii. 29; Ezek. xxxi. 10; Dan. xi. 12; Hos. xiii. 6: (f) Ps. ci. 5; Prov. xxi. 4 (as against Ps. cxix. 32; Isa. lx. 5, where this idiom, too, is used in a good sense).

[5] Cf. Ps. cxix. 70; Isa. vi. 10.

[6] Cf. Lev. xxvi. 41 (H); Deut. x. 16, xxx. 6; Jer. iv. 4, ix. 25; Ezek. xliv. 7, 9 (corresponding to the similar metaphor in connexion with the lips and the ear, Exod. vi. 12, 30 (both P); Jer. vi. 10): also Lam. iii. 65.

and, on the other, to the fact that the heart has turned to stone or, as we should say, has become 'petrified'.[1] Accordingly, if Yahweh's ideal standard of behaviour is to become an actuality, it is necessary for man to undergo a radical change of heart with all that this implies as to the transformation of his character.[2] In short, the fundamental need is for 'a new heart' and (what obviously amounts to the same thing) 'a new רוּחַ';[3] and one must learn to pray in the words of the psalmist:[4]

> Create for me a clean heart, O God;
> And make new within me a steadfast רוּחַ.

When all is said and done, however, this can only be achieved as man's 'stony' heart is shattered, and he numbers himself with those whose heart is 'broken' and whose רוּחַ is 'crushed', thus taking sides with all the stricken and oppressed amongst his fellow men;[5] i.e. he must also learn to say with the psalmist,[6]

> My sacrifice, O God, is a broken רוּחַ;
> A broken and a contrite heart, O God, Thou wilt not despise.

When this takes place, there will be a new and vital relationship between Israel and God, i.e. what Jeremiah calls the new covenant which is to be inscribed upon the heart;[7]

---

[1] Ezek. xi. 19, xxxvi. 26; Zech. vii. 12.

[2] Cf. 1 Sam. x. 9.

[3] Ezek. xviii. 31, xxxvi. 26: cf. Jer. xxxii. 39; Ezek. xi. 19, as cited above, p. 80, n. 5.

[4] Ps. li. 12 (EVV. 10), as quoted above, p. 36.

[5] Cf. carefully with each other Pss. xxxiv. 19 (EVV. 18), li. 19 (EVV. 17), as quoted above in the text, lxix. 21 (EVV. 20), cxlvii. 3; Isa. lxi. 1; Jer. xxiii. 9; Ezek. vi. 9: also Lev. xxvi. 41 (H); Ps. cvii. 12.

[6] Ps. li. 19 (EVV. 17). Cf. Joel ii. 13; also (for the general principle) Lam. iii. 41. In the passage quoted the traditional rendering of the English Versions follows the vocalization of M.T. in the case of the first word, i.e. yielding 'The sacrifices of God are . . .' instead of 'My sacrifice, O God, is . . .': but see, for example, H. Gunkel, H.K. (1926), *in loc.*, also R.S.V. mgn.

[7] xxxi. 31–34: cf. (apropos this new and vital relationship) Deut. xxx. 6, as cited above, p. 85, n. 6. The writer hopes to deal with the principle of the בְּרִית and its related terminology in an immediate sequel to the work referred to above, p. 82, n. 1, i.e. in a study to be entitled *The Vital Importance of the Covenant in the Thought of Ancient Israel.* A first draft of one section

for, as the unknown prophet of the Exile says, speaking in the name of Yahweh:[1]

> Thus saith the high and exalted One,
>   That abideth for ever, whose Name is holy:
> 'On high and in holiness I dwell,
>   But also with the contrite and the lowly in רוּחַ;
> Bringing life to the רוּחַ of the lowly,
>   Bringing life to the heart of the contrite.'

All in all, therefore, it is little wonder that the Israelite sage advised his pupil to keep watch over his heart on the ground that it is there that the springs of life are to be found, i.e.:[2]

> Above everything guard thy heart,
>   For it is the well-spring of life.[3]

The matter may not be left there, however, for this raises the whole question as to what exactly the thoughtful (or, at least, the orthodox) Israelite meant, when he spoke in this way of 'life'—and, what is more, 'death'.

IV

In the foregoing pages we have been concerned with the fact that in Israelite thought man is conceived, not so much in dual fashion as 'body' and 'soul', but synthetically as a unit of vital power or (in current terminology) a psychophysical organism. That is to say, the various members and secretions of the body, such as the bones, the heart, the bowels, and the kidneys, as well as the flesh and the blood, can all be thought of as revealing psychical properties. Indeed, we may recall the fact that this vital power is thought to reach far beyond the mere contour of the body; for, as the present writer has pointed out elsewhere, it is

of this study, dealing with the terms חֶסֶד and חָסִיד, can now be found in *Interpretationes ad Vetus Testamentum pertinentes* (S. Mowinckel *Festschrift*) = *Nor.T.T.* lvi, 1.–2. Hefte (1955), pp. 100–12.

[1] Isa. lvii. 15, as quoted above, p. 36. Cf. the language of Pss. xxii. 27 (EVV. 26), lxix. 33 (EVV. 32); and see below, p. 97, n. 1.

[2] Prov. iv. 23: cf. xiv. 30.

[3] EVV. 'For out of it are the issues of life': but cf. now R.S.V.

even found to be present in such 'extensions' of the personality as the spoken and, no doubt, the written word, one's name, one's property, and (most important of all) one's offspring.[1]

At death, however, the unity of this whole is broken up; the organism as a centre of vital power is destroyed. Nevertheless, this does not mean a man's complete extinction. For some time at least he may live on as an individual (apart from his possible survival within the social unit) in such scattered elements of his personality as the bones,[2] the blood,[3] and the name.[4] Thus death is to be explained in terms of life. It is a weak and indeed, in so far as it marks the final disintegration of one's נֶפֶשׁ, the weakest form of life; for it involves a complete scattering of one's vital power. As already observed, this is seen to drain away, so that it may be said of the so-called Suffering Servant, for example, that he 'empties' his נֶפֶשׁ as an offering to 'Death', just as one's נֶפֶשׁ is said to be 'poured out', when one is faint with sickness or hunger; and so on.[5] In short, we have to recall that at death man is like water which has been spilt upon the ground and cannot be gathered up again.[6]

This conception of death as a weak form of life may also be seen in the fact that man is further pictured as living on, a mere shadow of his former self, in company with the רְפָאִים in the underworld of Sheol. This general name for

---

[1] See *The One and the Many in the Israelite Conception of God*, pp. 5 ff., 2nd edit., pp. 1 ff.

[2] Cf. 2 Kings xiii. 20 f. This may explain why the burning of one's bones was regarded with special horror: cf. Amos ii. 1; also Gen. xxxviii. 24 (J); Lev. xx. 14, xxi. 9 (H); Joshua vii. 25 (JE); 2 Kings xxiii. 16 ff. See above, p. 69.

[3] Cf. Gen. iv. 10 (J), xxxvii. 26 (J); Job xvi. 18; Isa. xxvi. 21; Ezek. xxiv. 7 f. See above, pp. 71 f.

[4] Cf. the legislation providing for the levirate marriage, and the fact that Absalom set up a memorial to himself in the neighbourhood of Jerusalem because, as we are expressly told, he had no (surviving?) son to perpetuate his name. Deut. xxv. 5 f.; 2 Sam. xviii. 18 (cf. xiv. 27).

[5] Cf. (a) Isa. liii. 12; also Ps. cxli. 8 (as R.V. mgn.): (b) Job xxx. 16; Lam. ii. 12. See above, pp. 8 f.

[6] Cf. 2 Sam. xiv. 14, as above, p. 9, n. 5.

the dead (or, perhaps, the *élite* among the dead),[1] which is peculiar to the west Semitic area, is of disputed derivation; but it is commonly associated with √רפה, 'to sink (or relax)', and is then taken to denote weakness or loss of energy.[2] Whether this be correct or not (and, indeed, it now seems to be untenable),[3] there can be no doubt that in

---

[1] Cf., for example, A. Lods, *Israël des origines au milieu du VIIIᵉ siècle* (1930), p. 134, E.T. by S. H. Hooke, *Israel from its Beginnings to the Middle of the Eighth Century* (1932), p. 117; 'De quelques récits de voyage au pays des morts', *Institut de France: Académie des Inscriptions et Belles-Lettres* (1940), pp. 4 ff.

[2] Although the connexion is not yet clear, it seems likely that the term in question is the same as that which is used to denote an ancient race of giants who were reputed to have occupied certain parts of Palestine. Cf. Gen. xiv. 5, xv. 20 (J); Deut. ii. 10 f., 20 f., iii. 11; 2 Sam. v. 18, 22, xxi. 16, 18, 20, 22, &c. Accordingly, the supposed association with √רפה has been explained in this case on some such ground, for example, as that it denotes a people who were dead and gone, and so were but dimly known. Cf. F. Schwally, *Das Leben nach dem Tode nach den Vorstellungen des alten Israel, &c.* (1892), p. 64, n. 1. This, however, is extremely doubtful: cf., for example, E. (P.) Dhorme, *L'Évolution religieuse d'Israël. I: La Religion des Hébreux nomades* (1937), pp. 122 f., and the works cited in the following note.

[3] M. J. Lagrange, *Études sur les religions sémitiques*, 2nd edit. rev. (1905), pp. 318 f., suggests that it may mean 'healers', as from √רפא, 'to heal', and compares the ἥρως ἰατρός of Athens. The term occurs in the Phoenician inscriptions, but they give no help on this point: cf. G. A. Cooke, *A Text-book of North-Semitic Inscriptions* (1903), 4.8, 5.8. On the other hand, support for a derivation from √רפא, rather than √רפה, appears to be forthcoming from the Ras Shamra tablets (fourteenth century B.C.) with their reference to the *rp'um*, as discussed originally by Ch. Virolleaud, in *Comptes rendus de l'Académie des Inscriptions et Belles-Lettres* (1939), pp. 638–40, 'Les Rephaïm', *R.E.S.* (1940), pp. 77–83, 'Les Rephaïm: fragments de poèmes de Ras Shamra', *Syria* xxii (1941), pp. 1–30; and by R. Dussaud, *Les Découvertes de Ras Shamra (Ugarit) et l'Ancien Testament*, 2nd edit. rev. (1941), pp. 185–8, who follows Lods (cf. the preceding note) in stressing the likelihood that originally the term רְפָאִים denoted the *élite* among the dead. Opinions differ on points of interpretation and indeed (as will be seen from the final reference in this note) on the question of etymology; but it is usual to relate the Ugaritic term to the Hebrew רְפָאִים and to explain it as being derived from √rp' = √רפא in either an active or a passive sense. Thus, on the one hand, we have the suggestion that the term should be construed with an active force as having reference to certain cultic functionaries who were designated 'healers' because they were responsible for the fertility of the soil. Cf. J. Gray, 'The Rephaim', *P.E.Q.* (1949), pp. 127–39, '*Dtn* and *Rp'um* in Ancient Ugarit', *P.E.Q.* (1952), pp. 39–41, and *The Legacy of Canaan: The Ras Shamra Texts and their Relevance to the Old Testament*, S.V.T. iii (1957), pp. 153 ff. Others, however, interpret the role of the *rp'um* with

actual use the term does suggest a relative weakness on the part of the dead as compared with the state of the living. Thus in a song of triumph over the death of some tyrant, whose name we can now only conjecture, the prophet exultingly cries:[1]

> Sheol beneath is astir for thee
> To greet thy coming;
> Rousing for thee the רְפָאִים,
> All of earth's leaders;
> Raising up from their thrones
> All kings of nations.
> They all of them make response,
> Addressing thee thus:
> 'Thou too art made weak as we;
> Thou art made like us!'

Further, this underworld of Sheol, which swallows up mankind like some insatiable monster,[2] is thought of as more probability as that of chthonic deities or, better perhaps, agents of the Underworld; and in this connexion it has been suggested that the term under discussion, like the Hebrew רְפָאִים, is connected with √rpʾ = √רפא in its primary meaning 'to join' (cf. رَفَ, 'to mend': رَفَ, 'union') and is to be explained in a passive sense as originally denoting those who are 'joined' or 'massed' together in the community of the dead. Cf. H. L. Ginsberg, *The Legend of King Keret: A Canaanite Epic of the Bronze Age*, *B.A.S.O.R.* Supplementary Studies 2–3 (1946), p. 41; followed by G. R. Driver, *Canaanite Myths and Legends*, p. 10, n. 2. This is particularly interesting in view of the suggestion made by R. Gordis, 'Studies in Hebrew Roots of Contrasted Meanings', *J.Q.R.* xxvii (1936–7), pp. 55 f., that √רפא and √רפה have a common origin, and that we should think in terms of a semantic polarization giving the opposed meaning of (*a*) strength, and (*b*) weakness. The foregoing approach to the question at issue may also be examined in a wider context by consulting (i) K. Stendahl, 'Gamla Testamentets föreställningar om helandet. Rafaʾ-utsagorna i kontext och ideologi', *S.E.Å.* xv (1950), pp. 5–33, and especially (ii) J. Hempel, *Heilung als Symbol und Wirklichkeit im biblischen Schrifttum*, N.A.W.G. 1958: 3. Recently, however, the whole subject has been rendered more complicated by the theory that this Ugaritic term should be regarded as a loan-word from the Accadian RUBĀʾUM, RUBÛ, in its use to denote a 'noble' or 'prince': cf. J. Aistleitner, *Wörterbuch der ugaritischen Sprache*, ed. O. Eissfeldt, B.V.S.A.W.L. 106: 3 (1963), s.v., and note what is said above about the רְפָאִים as the *élite* among the dead.

[1] Isa. xiv. 9 f. Cf. lix. 10: and see further Job xxvi. 5; Ps. lxxxviii. 11 (EVV. 10); Prov. ii. 18, ix. 18, xxi. 16; Isa. xxvi. 14, 19.

[2] Cf. Isa. v. 14; Hab. ii. 5: also Num. xvi. 30–34 (JE); Prov. i. 12, xxvii. 20, xxx. 15 f.

a great pit[1] which lies, not only deep beneath the surface
of the earth, but also beneath the waters of the great
cosmic sea on which the whole world rests, and in which
are sunk the bases of earth's mountains as the very pillars
of heaven.[2] To die, therefore, is to find oneself sinking

---

[1] Hebrew שַׁחַת: cf. Job xvii. 13 f.; Ps. xvi. 10; Isa. xxxviii. 17 f.; Ezek.
xxviii. 8, &c. Cf. B.D.B. and K.B., s.v.; but, for a defence of the rendering
'corruption' in most if not all of the relevant passages, see E. F. Sutcliffe,
The Old Testament and the Future Life (1946), 2nd edit. rev. (1947), pp. 39 f.,
76 ff. In keeping with this thought of a great pit it has been suggested that the
term שְׁאוֹל is derived from √שׁעל as actually denoting a 'hollow': cf. the use
of the noun שֹׁעַל to denote the 'hollow' of the hand. See further B.D.B., s.v.,
adding, for example, E. Sellin, *Theologie des Alten Testaments* (1933), p. 79;
but note that this view is now generally abandoned. For recent attempts to
solve the problem, see (i) L. Köhler, in *T.Z.* ii (1946), pp. 71–74, and *J.S.S.*
i (1956), pp. 19 f., who sees here the formation of a noun from √שׁאה 'to be
desolate' or 'to be in ruins' (cf. Isa. vi. 11) by the established practice of
affixing ל, the name thus implying the thought of the Underworld as a place
of desolation and decay: (ii) W. Baumgartner, in *T.Z.* ii (1946), pp. 233–5,
who prefers to follow W. F. Albright, 'Mesopotamian Elements in Canaanite
Eschatology', in *Oriental Studies* (Paul Haupt *Festschrift*), ed. C. Adler and
A. Ember (1926), pp. 143–54, specifically pp. 151 f., and sees, rather, a word
of Mesopotamian origin corresponding to the Babylonian place-name
Shu'āra, the home of Tammuz in the Underworld, which came to be used of
the Underworld as a whole.

[2] See altogether Gen. vii. 11, viii. 2 (P), xlix. 25; Exod. xx. 4 (cf. Deut.
iv. 18); Deut. xxxii. 22, xxxiii. 13; 2 Sam. xxii. 5 f., 8, 16 (corresponding to
Ps. xviii. 5 f., 8, 16 f. (EVV. 4 f., 7, 15 f.)); Job xxvi. 10 f., xxxviii. 6, 16 f.;
Pss. xxiv. 2, xxxiii. 7, lxix. 16 (EVV. 15), lxxi. 20, lxxxviii. 5–8 (EVV. 4–7),
cxxxvi. 6; Prov. viii. 24–29; Jonah ii. 6 f. (as quoted later in the text);
also Ezek. xxvi. 19–21. Cf., too, J. Kroll, *Gott und Hölle: Der Mythos vom
Descensuskampfe* (1932), p. 325, n. 2. Although the present writer was forced
into accepting this view by an independent examination of the data, it is to
be observed that it has not been without its advocates elsewhere. Cf. Sutcliffe, op. cit., pp. 45 f., who in the first edition of his work rejected the view
in question as being too improbable even for the primitive mind. Sutcliffe's
argument, however, quite failed to take into consideration all the relevant
facts, and it was valid only in so far as it opposed the view that the earth was
thought of as *floating* upon the cosmic sea. Accordingly it is no matter for
surprise to find that in the second edition of Sutcliffe's work, published only
a year later, these pages were rewritten in favour of the view which he had
previously rejected. Altogether, then, the evidence should be unmistakable,
however difficult it may be on a literal approach to harmonize with such a
cosmology all the different metaphorical language concerning the dead: cf.,
for example, the more non-committal discussion of this point in (*a*) Pedersen,
Israel I–II, pp. 358 ff., E.T., pp. 460 ff.: (*b*) the important monograph by
C. Barth, *Die Errettung vom Tode in den individuellen Klage- und Dankliedern*

beneath these waters into a veritable cistern[1] or well;[2] and to be with the רְפָאִים in Sheol is to be 'beneath the waters and their inhabitants'.[3] As one writer of the Old Testament graphically expresses it (in a psalm which, happily, has been preserved through its accommodation to the book of Jonah):[4]

> I called from out of my distress
> Unto Yahweh, and He answered me.

des Alten Testaments (1947), pp. 80 ff., which, incidentally, discusses the whole subject in the light of the Assyro-Babylonian parallels, and is altogether a much more reliable guide in this connexion than A. Heidel, *The Gilgamesh Epic and Old Testament Parallels*; cf., for example, W. Baumgartner, in *B.O.* iv (1947), pp. 143–5: (*c*) P. Reymond, *L'Eau, sa vie, et sa signification dans l'Ancien Testament*, S.V.T. vi (1958), pp. 212 ff. See also A. J. Wensinck, *The Ocean in the Literature of the Western Semites*, V.K.A.W.A., N.R. xix. 2 (1918), esp. pp. 15 ff., 40 ff.; and cf. now Schmitt, *Leben in den Weisheitsbüchern Job, Sprüche und Jesus Sirach*, pp. 159 f.

[1] Pss. xxx. 4 (EVV. 3), lxxxviii. 4 f. (EVV. 3 f.); Prov. i. 12; Isa. xiv. 15, xxxviii. 18; Ezek. xxxi. 16; and often.

[2] Ps. lxix. 16 (EVV. 15). Cf. Ps. lv. 24 (EVV. 23); also, as regards the 'mouth' of the well, Ps. cxli. 7.

[3] i.e. the fish and other marine creatures, Job xxvi. 5: cf. Exod. xx. 4; Deut. iv. 18. Accordingly the reader ought, perhaps, to be warned that such a diagram as that in *D.B.* i, p. 503b, is somewhat misleading. Cf. now (i.e. since these words were first written) Barth, loc. cit.

[4] Jonah ii. 3 ff. (EVV. 2 ff.). For two outstanding parallels to the highly picturesque language of the following lines with their employment of a metaphor which in varying degree is a feature of Hebrew psalmody, see Pss. lxix and lxxxviii. Cf., too, Ps. xviii (= 2 Sam. xxii), as discussed in *Sacral Kingship in Ancient Israel*, pp. 107 ff. As regards the translation which is given above in the text, note that in verse 4 מְצוּלָה has been omitted on both metrical and grammatical grounds as a gloss upon נָהָר, which is used here in a specialized sense with reference to the primeval ocean: cf., for example, Pss. xxiv. 2, xciii. 3, and see *Sacral Kingship in Ancient Israel*, p. 24, n. 2, p. 58, n. 3. Further, as is now generally recognized, the first two words of verse 7 should be construed with the last three words of verse 6 so as to form a complete 3:2 line. Finally, the text of the relative clause in verse 7, which is rendered above by 'whose bars were to be about me for ever', is sometimes viewed with suspicion through taking the Hebrew as necessarily having a past significance and, therefore, as being irreconcilable with the deliverance which the psalm so clearly celebrates. Accordingly, attempts have been made to emend the text, as in the suggestion that (following LXX and V) one should read בְּדֵי for בַּעֲדִי so as to secure the rendering 'the land whose bars are everlasting bolts'. Cf. A. van Hoonacker, E.B. (1908); followed by J. A. Bewer, I.C.C. (1912), and G. W. Wade, W.C. (1925). However, such emendation is quite unnecessary; for the rendering of the Hebrew in terms of a relative clause, see G.K., § 155e.

Out of the belly of Sheol I cried;
　Thou didst hear my voice.
Thou hadst flung me ( ) amid the seas,
　So that the current surrounded me;
All Thy billows and Thy waves[1]
　Passed over me.
Yea, I thought that I had been swept
　Out of Thy sight.
Howbeit I can gaze once more
　Upon Thy holy Temple!

Water encompassed me up to the neck (נֶפֶשׁ);[2]
　The deep surrounded me.
Reeds became entwined about my head
　At the bases of the mountains.
I went down to the land whose bars
　Were to be about me for ever.

[1] The fact that the psalmist can refer to '*Thy* billows' and '*Thy* waves' (cf. Pss. xlii. 8 (EVV. 7), lxxxviii. 8 (EVV. 7)) is to be explained initially in terms of Yahweh's subjection of the cosmic sea at the time of the Creation and His continuing control of its restless waters; so that even in the case of so personal a reference, as also, of course, in the more impersonal language used elsewhere (e.g. Ps. lxix, as cited in the preceding note), there is a cosmological basis to the psalmist's obviously metaphorical language. See further, for example, *Sacral Kingship in Ancient Israel*, pp. 54 ff.; and H. G. May, 'Some Cosmic Connotations of *Mayim Rabbîm*, "Many Waters" ', *J.B.L.* lxxiv (1955), pp. 9–21. An example of the common failure to do justice to this whole standpoint may be seen in the article by J. J. McGovern, 'The Waters of Death', *C.B.Q.* xxi (1959), pp. 350–8; for the 'rushing torrents and wadies of Palestine' to which McGovern refers as the supposed source of the metaphorical language under discussion would not have been seen in isolation but would have served as awesome reminders of the lurking power of the subterranean ocean: cf. B. Vawter, 'A Note on "The Waters beneath the Earth" ', *C.B.Q.* xxii (1960), pp. 71–73.

[2] C. R. Smith, *The Bible Doctrine of Man* (1951), p. 8, n. 1, is sceptical of the view that נֶפֶשׁ may denote 'throat' or 'neck', and, apropos this passage, finds it unlikely that 'a man sunk, like Jonah, to the "reeds" of the sea-bottom, would say "The waters compassed me even to the neck" '; but this is to overlook the fact that at this point in the psalm the author is describing afresh his descent to the Underworld, beginning anew with the way in which the waters had gradually closed over him as he sank down to the floor of the great cosmic sea on his way to the realm of the dead. For the divisions of the poem, see van Hoonacker, op. cit., p. 330, i.e.: 'Le morceau se divise en quatre parties. D'abord le thème (v. 3); puis trois sections vv. 4–5, 6–7, 8–10, dans lesquelles l'expression de la joie de la délivrance succède chaque fois à la remémoration des angoisses endurées; dans la section finale, 8–10, c'est l'expression de la joie surtout qui est développée.'

Yet Thou didst bring up my life from the Pit (שַׁחַת),
O Yahweh, my God!

Once inside this foul region of virtual annihilation,[1] the gates of the Underworld are locked fast upon one;[2] and there can be no return to former conditions in 'the land of the living',[3] nor indeed any fellowship with Yahweh—the Giver of Life.[4] In fact, for the most part it is a still and silent 'land of forgetfulness',[5] which even at its best is but a pale and gloomy reflection of the world of light and life which is Yahweh's special sphere; so that Job, for example, faced with the prospect of death, makes the following pathetic plea for a momentary respite from his suffering, i.e.:[6]

> Ere I go whence I shall not return,
>   To the land of darkness and deep shadow,
> The land of dusk-like gloom,
>   Of deep shadow and disorder,
> No brighter than the dusk!

Here, as in the P narrative of the Creation,[7] darkness and confusion are linked in striking contrast with the ordered world of light and life, for at death a man's vital power is

---

[1] Cf. the use of אֲבַדּוֹן (A.V. 'destruction', R.V. 'Abaddon' or 'Destruction') as a synonym for Sheol in Job xxvi. 6; Prov. xv. 11, xxvii. 20 (Q): see also Job xxviii. 22, xxxi. 12; Ps. lxxxviii. 12 (EVV. 11). Cf., too, Hos. xiii. 14.

[2] Cf. Job xxxviii. 17; Pss. ix. 14 (EVV. 13), cvii. 18; Isa. xxxviii. 10; Jonah ii. 7 (EVV. 6), as above in the text.

[3] Cf. Job vii. 9 f.; also 2 Sam. xii. 23; Job x. 21 f. (as quoted below in the text), xvi. 22; Prov. ii. 18 f.: and for 'the land of the living (*or* life)', see below, p. 107, n. 5.

[4] Cf. Pss. vi. 6 (EVV. 5), xxviii. 1, xxx. 10 (EVV. 9), lxxxviii. 11–13 (EVV. 10–12), cxv. 17, cxliii. 7; Isa. xxxviii. 11, 18: and for Yahweh as 'Giver of Life', see below, pp. 106 f. This is not to say, of course, that it was inconceivable that Yahweh should make His presence felt even in Sheol: cf. Ps. cxxxix. 8; Amos ix. 2.

[5] Ps. lxxxviii. 13 (EVV. 12). Cf. Ps. vi. 6 (EVV. 5); Eccles. ix. 10: and for the stillness and silence of the Underworld, see Job iii. 11–19; Pss. xxxi. 18 (EVV. 17), xciv. 17, cxv. 17.

[6] x. 21 f. Cf. Job xvii. 13, xxxviii. 17; Pss. lxxxviii. 7, 13 (EVV. 6, 12), cxliii. 3; Isa. lix. 10; Lam. iii. 6: also the association of light and life, as in Job iii. 20, xxxiii. 28, 30; Pss. xxxvi. 10 (EVV. 9), xlix. 20 (EVV. 19), lvi. 14 (EVV. 13).   [7] Gen. i. 1 ff.

found to be broken up in disorder, its unity shattered; and the result is that as an individual he drags on a relatively weak existence, which is as opposed to life in its fullness as darkness is to light.[1]

Moreover, just as death in the strict sense of the term is for the Israelite the weakest form of life, so any weakness in life is a form of death. This is a point of fundamental importance, which finds ready illustration in √היה.[2] Thus

---

[1] See further Pedersen, loc. cit.; Barth, op. cit., pp. 33 ff.; and (if used with discrimination) A. M. Gierlich, *Der Lichtgedanke in den Psalmen* (1940), pp. 130 ff., 159 ff. I am thus unable to agree with G. R. Driver, in *Wisdom in Israel and in the Ancient Near East* (H. H. Rowley *Festschrift*), ed. M. Noth and D. W. Thomas, S.V.T. iii (1955), p. 76, that in the passage quoted the thought of disorder (cf. EVV. 'without any order') is alien to the context: cf. R.S.V., 'gloom and chaos', which rightly suggests a condition similar to that which, for the writer of Gen. i. 1 ff., prevailed before the Creation.

[2] The treatment of this point which follows in the text is based upon an independent examination of all the occurrences of the root in the Old Testament; but the reader should also consult (paying due attention to the parallels which are available in the other Semitic languages) W. W. Graf Baudissin, *Adonis und Ešmun: Eine Untersuchung zur Geschichte des Glaubens an Auferstehungsgötter und an Heilgötter* (1911), esp. pp. 385 ff., 'Alttestamentliches *ḥajjīm* „Leben" in der Bedeutung von „Glück" ', in *Festschrift Eduard Sachau*, ed. G. Weill (1915), pp. 143–61; F. Nötscher, *Altorientalischer und alttestamentlicher Auferstehungsglauben* (1926), pp. 17 ff., 133 ff.; M. A. Canney, 'The Meaning of "Salvation" ', *Theology* xv (1927), pp. 64–73; and the articles by G. Bertram, R. Bultmann, and G. von Rad, s.v. ζάω, ζωή, &c., in *Th.W.N.T.* ii (1935), pp. 833–77, e.g. 'Leben und Tod im AT.', pp. 844–50 (von Rad), 'Der Lebensbegriff des AT.', pp. 850–3 (Bultmann): also, in general, Pedersen, op. cit., pp. 116 ff., 353 ff., E.T., pp. 153 ff., 453 ff. L. Dürr, *Die Wertung des Lebens im Alten Testament und im antiken Orient* (1926); E. Sellin, *Theologie des Alten Testaments*, pp. 14 ff., 76 ff., 129 ff.; J. Hempel, *Gott und Mensch im Alten Testament*, B.W.A.N.T. iii. 2, 2nd edit. rev. (1936), pp. 197 ff., and now *Heilung als Symbol und Wirklichkeit im biblischen Schrifttum* (as cited above, p. 89, n. 3); H. Bergema, *De boom des levens in Schrift en historie* (1938), pp. 526 f.; O. Procksch, 'Der Lebensgedanke im Alten Testament', *C.W.* iv (1938), pp. 145 ff., 193 ff.; A. T. Nikolainen, *Der Auferstehungsglaube in der Bibel und ihrer Umwelt*, A.A.S.F., B XLIX, 3, i (1944), pp. 113 ff.; and especially Barth, op. cit., *passim*.

For the importance of recognizing the principle under discussion as governing much of the picturesque language of the Psalter (and, occasionally, other parts of the Old Testament), see H. Gunkel, *Ausgewählte Psalmen*, 4th edit. rev. (1917), pp. 212 ff.; H.K. (1926), p. 62 (i.e. on Ps. xviii. 7c–20), and *Einleitung in die Psalmen*, ed. J. Begrich (1933), pp. 184 ff.; Pedersen, op. cit., pp. 363 ff., E.T., pp. 466 ff.; G. Widengren, *The Accadian and Hebrew Psalms of Lamentation as Religious Documents* (1937), pp. 121 f., 239 ff.; and especially Barth, op. cit., *passim*. See also the special application

the verb *Qal*, i.e. חַי or חָיָה, 'to live', is used idiomatically, not only of '*sur*vival',[1] nor even simply of '*re*vival' as restoration from death in the normal sense of the latter term,[2] but also of 'revival' as recovery from bodily weakness of any kind. Thus it is said of Joshua's followers, for example, that, after they had been circumcised, they remained where they were in camp 'until they *lived*', i.e. until they recovered (EVV. 'till they were whole').[3] Indeed, this method of

of this principle which is reproduced in the present writer's essay on 'The Rôle of the King in the Jerusalem Cultus', in *The Labyrinth*, ed. S. H. Hooke (as cited above, p. 28, n. 4), pp. 98 ff., and, better, *Sacral Kingship in Ancient Israel*, pp. 97 ff.

Further, it is to be observed that the phenomenon under discussion has something of a parallel amongst the so-called 'primitives' of the present day. Cf., for example, W. H. R. Rivers, 'The Primitive Conception of Death', in *Psychology and Ethnology* (as cited above, p. 2, n. 3), pp. 36–50, esp. pp. 39 ff.; and A. M. Hocart, *The Progress of Man* (1933), pp. 136 ff., through which the writer's attention was first drawn to the seeming analogy. However, this had already been observed by E. Samter, *Volkskunde im altsprachlichen Unterricht, I: Homer* (1923), pp. 102 ff. (cf. Kroll, op. cit., p. 248), who gives a number of suggested parallels. Cf., too, Gunkel–Begrich, op. cit., pp. 187 f.; and W. Baumgartner, 'Der Auferstehungsglaube im Alten Orient', *Z.M.R.* xlviii (1933), pp. 193–214 (as cited by Barth, op. cit., p. 16, and now reproduced with additional comments in *Zum Alten Testament und seiner Umwelt* (1959), pp. 124–46). At the same time great caution is necessary here; for the parallel, while helpful, easily lends itself to over-emphasis.

Finally, since the publication of the first edition of this monograph the importance of studying the use of √חיה as a starting point for tracing the way in which the belief in a resurrection came into being and gradually found acceptance in Israel has been recognized by R. Martin-Achard, *De la mort à la résurrection d'après l'Ancien Testament* (1956), E.T. by J. P. Smith, *From Death to Life. A Study of the Development of the Doctrine of the Resurrection in the Old Testament* (1960); but I must say that it comes a little hard to find myself cited as sharing the view that the belief in the resurrection of the dead stemmed from the myth of the dying and rising god regarded as the core of the Old Testament (op. cit., p. 158, E.T., pp. 199 f.), when the fact is that I am far from holding any such view and, indeed, embarked on the present monograph as the first step in an attempt to show *inter alia* that such a theory is far too narrowly conceived. Cf., for example, my comments in 'Living Issues in Biblical Scholarship: Divine Kingship and the Old Testament', *E.T.* lxii (1950–1), pp. 36–42, particularly p. 41b with its specific reference to the first edition of this work.

[1] e.g. Gen. xx. 7 (E), xliii. 8 (J); Exod. i. 16 (E), xxxiii. 20 (J); Num. **xiv.** 38 (P); Deut. iv. 33; 2 Kings vii. 4; and so often.

[2] e.g. 1 Kings xvii. 22; 2 Kings xiii. 21; Job xiv. 14.

[3] Joshua v. 8 (JE): cf. Num. xxi. 8 f. (JE), the serpent-bitten Israelites; 2 Kings i. 2, the illness of Ahaziah; viii. 8 f., the illness of Benhadad; **xx. 7,**

indicating a clearly recognized ebb and flow in one's vitality may be reinforced, as we have seen, by a reference to the absence or presence of רוּחַ; so that it may be said of Samson, for example, when he was faint with thirst after a particularly strenuous conflict with the Philistines, that, having succeeded by the aid of Yahweh in finding a spring, and having drunk of its waters, 'his רוּחַ returned, and he *lived* (EVV. "and he revived")'.[1] Such illustrations, which may be multiplied,[2] serve to show that the familiar expression יְחִי הַמֶּלֶךְ (EVV. 'God save the king': mgn. 'Heb. *Let the king live*')[3] is really equivalent to our toasting the king's 'health'; and even the rare addition of the phrase לְעוֹלָם (EVV. 'for ever')[4] is not so much the expression of a wish that the king may actually 'live for ever' as that he may ever enjoy good health. Indeed, in the light of the common Israelite conception of man as a whole we may go further and say that it carries with it the wish that the king may

---

and Isa. xxxviii. 9, 21, the illness of Hezekiah. In the following passages the suggestion of a 'revival' in the sense under discussion, though present, tends to be outweighed by the thought of 'survival': 2 Sam. i. 10, the grievously wounded Saul; xii. 22, the illness of David's first child by Bath-sheba; 2 Kings viii. 10, 14, the illness of Benhadad (as above); xx. 1, and Isa. xxxviii. 1, the illness of Hezekiah (as above). Cf., too, the use of the *Hiph'il* in 2 Kings v. 7 (as referred to below, p. 101, n. 3, and p. 108, n. 2), i.e. the incident of Naaman's leprosy.

[1] Judges xv. 19: cf. Gen. xlv. 27 (E), and see above, p. 25. Cf., too, the use of the *Hiph'il* in Isa. lvii. 15, as quoted above, pp. 36 and 87, and below, p. 101. What is more, there is a corresponding use with the term for 'heart' in Pss. xxii. 27 (EVV. 26), lxix. 33 (EVV. 32): cf. again the use of the *Hiph'il* in Isa. lvii. 15, i.e. in parallelism with both רוּחַ and לֵב, and see above, p. 87, n. 1. This is rather different from the comparatively frequent use with נֶפֶשׁ, where the emphasis tends to rest upon 'survival': i.e. Gen. xii. 13 (J), xix. 20 (J); 1 Kings xx. 32; Jer. xxxviii. 17, 20; Ezek. xiii. 19. Cf. (a) the *Pi'ēl* in 1 Kings xx. 31; Ps. xxii. 30 (EVV. 29); Ezek. xiii. 18, 19, xviii. 27: and (b) the *Hiph'il* in Gen. xix. 19 (J). Nevertheless, the use of the *Qal* in Ps. cxix. 175 should be compared with the frequent use of the *Pi'ēl* (with an obvious emphasis upon the thought of 'revival') elsewhere in this psalm, as referred to below, p. 99, n. 4; and there is a striking exception to the foregoing rule in the case of Isa. lv. 3, as quoted below, pp. 98 f.

[2] i.e. as indicated in the two previous notes.

[3] 1 Sam. x. 24; 2 Sam. xvi. 16; 2 Kings xi. 12; 2 Chron. xxiii. 11: cf. the expanded form in 1 Kings i. 25, 34, 39.

[4] i.e. with the expanded form in 1 Kings i. 31: cf. Neh. ii. 3.

enjoy unceasing prosperity;[1] for it must be borne in mind that, at the level with which we are dealing, a man's property was thought to form an important 'extension' of his personality, i.e. it was axiomatic that a man's 'life' consisted in the abundance of the things which he possessed.[2] There may have been (and in fact, of course, there were) limits to the means which it was thought legitimate to adopt in order to acquire them, but that is not our immediate concern. The point to be noted here is that when the Israelite teacher, in warning his pupil against bribery, asserts that the man who goes so far as to be greedy of gain ultimately destroys his own household, whereas the man who hates such gifts 'will *live*', the context shows quite clearly that he is using √חיה in the verb *Qal* with a strongly material connotation to indicate that this type of man will enjoy a *prosperous* life.[3] At the same time (as this passage itself indicates) there were those in Israel who realized that man does not 'live' on the basis of bread alone, but that the ultimate foundation for a truly prosperous life is to be found in obedience to and fellowship with Yahweh,[4] i.e. the '*Living* God' (אֵל חַי);[5] and again √חיה in the verb *Qal* is sufficient of itself to express this thought of life in its fullness, as when the prophet thus addresses his compatriots on behalf of the 'Holy One' of Israel:[6]

[1] P. A. H. de Boer, '„Vive le roi!" ', *V.T.* v (1955), pp. 225 ff., quite fails to do justice to my argument, when he ignores the fact that I thus go on to make the point that יְחִי הַמֶּלֶךְ really implies more than toasting the king's health; obviously I could not agree more that 'l'acclamation Vive le roi! n'est pas équivalente à un simple souhait pour la bonne santé du roi' (p. 228). On the other hand, I am wholly unconvinced by his attempt to prove that the jussive has the force of an indicative, so that the whole expression is simply an acknowledgement that the king has the power of life and death over his subjects.

[2] The reader will observe that the writer has in mind the contrast afforded by Luke xii. 15, and that he finds the rendering of the standard English Versions wholly acceptable; in fact it hits the nail squarely upon the head!

[3] Prov. xv. 27.

[4] Cf. Deut. viii. 3. See further Deut. iv. 1, v. 30 (33), viii. 1, xvi. 20, xxx. 16, 19 (as cited below, p. 105, n. 5): also Lev. xviii. 5 (H); Neh. ix. 29.

[5] See below, p. 106, n. 4.

[6] Isa. lv. 1–3a: cf. verse 5b. In this case the parallelism with the preceding

Ho, everyone that thirsteth, come ye to the waters;
  And whoso hath no money, come, buy and eat!
Yea, come, buy wine and milk
  Without money and without price!
Why spend ye money for that which is not bread,
  And your earnings for that which satisfieth not?
O hearken to Me, that ye may eat what is good,
  May enjoy with your whole being (נֶפֶשׁ) the richest of food!
Incline your ear, and come unto Me;
  Hearken, that with your whole being (נֶפֶשׁ) ye may *live*!

Similarly the *Pi'ēl* of the verb admits a wide range of meaning, which in its intensive force goes far beyond the simple thought of merely preserving life.[1] In the first place, for example, it is used of fostering or enhancing life, i.e. with reference to the rearing of cattle or sheep,[2] or in making the point that wisdom enriches the lives of those who possess it.[3] What is more, it is also used of restoring life; and again it is important to note that this involves not so much a restoration from death in the narrow sense of the term, but rather a deliverance from adversity and a consequent reinforcement of one's vitality or enlivening of the whole personality—whether that of an individual or that of the social body. A typical case is that in which the psalmist pleads with Yahweh for deliverance from the assaults of his enemies by saying:[4]

For Thy Name's sake, Yahweh, do Thou cause me to *live*!
In Thy righteousness free my being (נֶפֶשׁ) from distress!

line is specially instructive; and it is significant that LXX here renders the verbal form under discussion, not by ζήσεται merely, but by ζήσεται ἐν ἀγαθοῖς! (Incidentally, for it makes no difference to the point at issue, the writer is unable to follow the argument that because verse 3a repeats the thought of verse 2b it must be a gloss: cf., for example, G. H. Box, *The Book of Isaiah* (1916), *in loc.*, following Duhm, Cheyne, and Marti.)

[1] e.g. Gen. xii. 12 (J); Exod. i. 17, 18, 22 (E); Deut. xx. 16; Joshua ix. 15; Judges xxi. 14; 1 Sam. xxvii. 9, 11; 1 Kings xx. 31; 2 Kings vii. 4; Neh. ix. 6; and so often.

[2] 2 Sam. xii. 3; Isa. vii. 21: cf. perhaps Hos. xiv. 8 (EVV. 7) and the consonantal text of Zech. x. 9 (vide LXX).

[3] Eccles. vii. 12.

[4] Ps. cxliii. 11: cf. Pss. xxx. 4 (EVV. 3), xli. 3 (EVV. 2), lxxi. 20 (Q), cxix. 25, 37, 40, 50, 88, 93, 107, 149, 154, 156, 159; also perhaps cxxxviii. 7.

Here the parallelism itself is sufficient to reveal the force
of the verbal form under discussion; but it may be made
abundantly clear by comparing the earlier words of the
psalmist, i.e.:[1]

> For an enemy hath persecuted my being (נֶפֶשׁ);
> He hath ground my life (חַיָּה) into the dust,
>> Making me dwell in the dark like those long dead.

Similarly, when in time of adversity the life of the nation
itself is found to be at a low ebb, and resort is made to
public prayer, it is just such deliverance from death as a
restoration to greater vitality which is sought through the
medium of the *Pi'ēl*, as in the anxious inquiry:[2]

> Wilt Thou be angry with us for ever,
>> Extending Thy wrath to every generation?
> Wilt Thou not cause us to *live* again,
>> That Thy people may be glad in Thee?

In the same way a city in ruins is to be regarded as a lifeless
thing; but when unity is restored and the scattered elements
once more form an ordered whole, one is said to bring
the city to life again.[3] In Israelite thinking, however, this
example of the use of the *Pi'ēl* provides a parable of man;
for, as already pointed out, true life is only to be found in
that ordered functioning of the whole personality which
reveals itself in well-being of body and circumstance. Disorder is weakness, and weakness is death; unity is power,
and power is life.

The same force of √חיה is discernible again in the case of
the *Hiph'îl* of the verb, which is used to denote, not merely
the thought of simple '*sur*vival' in the sense 'to allow to live'

---

[1] Verse 3.

[2] Ps. lxxxv. 6 f. (EVV. 5 f.): cf. Pss. lxxi. 20 (K), lxxx. 19 (EVV. 18); Hos.
vi. 2. See also in general Deut. xxxii. 39 and 1 Sam. ii. 6, as quoted below,
p. 108.

[3] Cf. 1 Chron. xi. 8; Neh. iii. 34 (EVV. iv. 2). The integration which is
thus implied by the root under discussion is emphasized by W. F. Albright,
J.B.L. lxiii (1944), p. 222, n. 108, where it is suggested that its basic meaning
is 'to gather together'.

or 'to preserve' or 'to save',[1] but also the thought of a
'*revival*'—both in the narrow sense of restoring to life one
who has ceased to breathe[2] and in the broader sense of
restoring to normal health one who is weak and ailing.
Thus, when Naaman the Syrian sought the help of the king
of Israel that he might be cured of his leprosy, it was with
the aid of this verbal form that the latter asked in con-
sternation, 'Am I God (*or* a god) to cause to die (לְהָמִית)
and to make to *live* (לְהַחֲיוֹת)?'[3] Once again the force of the
verb is clear; the thought is obviously that of being made
'whole'—both in the sense of having one's health restored
and in the sense of arresting the disintegrating power of
death. Indeed, the idiom remains the same when, centuries
later, the great prophet of the Exile delivers the message
which has already attracted our attention on more than one
occasion, i.e.:[4]

> Thus saith the high and exalted One,
>   That abideth for ever, whose Name is holy:
> 'On high and in holiness I dwell,
>   But also with the contrite and the lowly in רוּחַ;
> *Bringing life to* the רוּחַ of the lowly,
>   *Bringing life to* the heart of the contrite.'

Finally, a similar connotation may be observed in the
case of the adjective חַי, 'living' or 'alive'.[5] Ideally, at least,
this implies the possession of one's powers in their totality,
as is clear from the words which the Israelite sage attributes
to the man who plots against his fellows:[6]

---

[1] e.g. Gen. vi. 19 f. (P), xix. 19 (J), xlv. 7 (E); Num. xxii. 33 (J), xxxi. 18
(P); Judges viii. 19; 2 Sam. viii. 2; and so comparatively often.

[2] 2 Kings viii. 1, 5.   [3] 2 Kings v. 7: cf. Isa. xxxviii. 16.

[4] Isa. lvii. 15: see above, pp. 36 and 87.

[5] e.g. (i) as a simple adjective, Gen. i. 24 (P), ii. 7 (J); Exod. iv. 18 (E);
Lev. xiii. 10 (i.e. of a raw spot in one's flesh: cf. 1 Sam. ii. 15), xiv. 4–7;
1 Sam. xv. 8; 2 Sam. xii. 18–23; 1 Kings xvii. 23, xxi. 15; Eccles. ix. 4; and
so often: (ii) as a noun, Gen. iii. 20 (J); Job xii. 10; Ps. cxliii. 2; Eccles. iv. 2;
Isa. viii. 19, xxxviii. 19; and so on, but much less frequently.

[6] Prov. i. 12: cf. Num. xvi. 30, 33 (JE); Ps. lv. 16 (EVV. 15); also Ps.
cxxiv. 3. Note, too, the suggestion of totality in the form חַי (corresponding
to the Arabic حَى) as used to denote a kin-group in 1 Sam. xviii. 18, and in

Let us swallow them, like Sheol, *alive* (חַי),
And *whole* (תְּמִים), like them that go down the Pit.

It thus suggests an active condition which is markedly
different from the comparatively inactive state of the
רְפָאִים in the underworld of Sheol, whose weakness is a
consequence of the disintegrating power of death. Indeed,
this force of the term finds ready illustration in the fact
that freshly flowing water, as compared with the static water
of a cistern, for example, is known idiomatically as 'living
water' (מַיִם חַיִּים).¹ It is not surprising, therefore, that it
could be used by itself to indicate a high degree of vitality,
as when it is said of the Hebrew women during the sojourn
in Egypt that they were so 'alive' (i.e. so full of life) that
they were wont to give birth to their children before the
midwife could arrive upon the scene.² Indeed, it is wholly

what appears to be the corresponding feminine form in 2 Sam. xxiii. 13 (as
against verse 11, where M.T. appears to be wrongly vocalized). Cf. S. R.
Driver, *Notes on the Hebrew Text of the Books of Samuel*, 2nd edit. rev. (1913),
in loc.: but see also Pedersen, op. cit., p. 391 (i.e. p. 37, n. 1), E.T., p. 505 (i.e.
p. 50, n. 1). It is likely that the latter form is to be recognized also in Ps.
lxviii. 11 (EVV. 10), as EVV. and R.S.V., and it may occur again in Ps. lxxiv.
19b (as A.V. and R.V. mgn.) but hardly in 19a (as A.V. and R.V. mgn.).
Cf., for example, M. Buttenwieser, *The Psalms: Chronologically Treated with
a New Translation* (1938), *in loc.*

¹ Gen. xxvi. 19 (J); Lev. xiv. 5, 6, 50, 51, 52, xv. 13; Num. xix. 17 (P);
Song of Sol. iv. 15; Jer. ii. 13, xvii. 13; Zech. xiv. 8. Note especially Jer. ii. 13.
² Exod. i. 19 (E): cf. N.H. חָיָה as used of a woman in childbirth. The
vocalization of M.T. seems quite anomalous: cf. the equally doubtful vocalization in 2 Sam. xx. 3, as discussed by S. R. Driver, op. cit., *in loc.*, and see now
G. R. Driver, 'Hebrew mothers (Exodus i 19)', *Z.A.W.* lxvii (1955), pp. 246–
8 (although, as I hope to show elsewhere, I cannot agree with the accompanying attempt to find a similar allusion in Ps. lxxviii. 50). On this analogy the
well-known idiom כָּעֵת חַיָּה (A.V. 'according to the time of life', R.V. 'when
the time (*or* season) cometh round', &c.) in Gen. xviii. 10, 14 (J), and 2 Kings
iv. 16, 17, appears to correspond to the English idiom, 'when the time is
(*or* was) ripe'. In view of the force which thus attaches to the term חַי it
may well be that one should follow K (אִישׁ חַי) rather than Q (אִישׁ חַיִל) in
2 Sam. xxiii. 20; and we may well be cautious even about emending the text
of Ps. xxxviii. 20 (EVV. 19) despite the tempting parallel in Ps. xxxv. 19, &c.
Similarly, in view of what has been said above with regard to the fact that
a man's 'life' was found to consist in the abundance of the things which he
possessed, it is possible that the occurrence of this term in 1 Sam. xxv. 6,
i.e. with reference to the obviously well-to-do Nabal as to 'him that liveth *in*

in line with such an extensive connotation of the term that the feminine form חַיָּה should have been used as a noun to denote not so much animal life in general[1] as wild animals, i.e. in opposition to the tame (and, therefore, comparatively lifeless) type,[2] and that ultimately this form came to be used in what we should call an abstract sense to denote the phenomenon of 'life' itself[3] and, what is more, even the thought of a renewal of life as in the 'enlivening' of one's hand.[4]

For the most part, however, the idea of 'life' is expressed by means of the masculine plural חַיִּים, which by its very form conveys a suggestion of intensity or expansiveness not to be divorced from the many and varied concrete expressions of 'life';[5] and it is the use of this form which adds most forcibly to our illustrations of the point under discussion. Thus it is used not only in a simple sense with reference to mere duration of one's personal existence,[6] but also in an

---

prosperity' (EVV.), is thoroughly idiomatic, and that the text is not to be regarded as corrupt. See, in general, S. R. Driver, op. cit., *in loc.*, and Gunkel, op. cit., *in loc.*

[1] e.g. Gen. viii. 17; Lev. xi. 2; Num. xxxv. 3 (P); Ps. civ. 25; Isa. xlvi. 1; and such visionary creatures as those of Ezek. i. 5, 13 ff.

[2] e.g. Gen. i. 25 (P), ii. 20 (J), vii. 14 (P); Lev. v. 2, xvii. 13 (H), xxvi. 22 (H); Deut. vii. 22; 2 Sam. xxi. 10; 2 Kings xiv. 9 (= 2 Chron. xxv. 18); Job xxxvii. 8; Pss. civ. 20, cxlviii. 10; Isa. lvi. 9; Ezek. xxxiii. 27; Hos. xiii. 8; Zeph. ii. 15; and so often.

[3] Only Job xxxiii. 18, 20, 22, 28, xxxvi. 14, xxxviii. 39; Pss. lxxiv. 19b (but see above, p. 101, n. 6), lxxviii. 50 (but see above, p. 102, n. 2), cxliii. 3 (as quoted above, p. 100); Ezek. vii. 13. Note, however, that in Job xxxiii. 20 and xxxviii. 39 it actually has the force of 'appetite'.

[4] Cf. Isa. lvii. 10: and note that Elisha's action in 2 Kings iv. 34 (which figures so prominently in H. W. Robinson's theory of a 'diffused consciousness', e.g. *Inspiration and Revelation in the Old Testament*, p. 72) finds ready and simple explanation in the light of this passage. Cf., too, the use of the cognate term מִחְיָה in 2 Chron. xiv. 12 (EVV. 13), where the implication appears to be that of being smitten 'beyond recovery' (cf. A.V., R.V. as against R.V. mgn., R.S.V.), and in Ezra ix. 8, 9, where the reference appears to be to the measure of 'recovery' (EVV., R.S.V. 'reviving') enjoyed by the post-exilic community.

[5] Cf. the alternative renderings 'life' or 'the living', which are noticed below, p. 107, nn. 3-6: and see further G.K., § 124*ad*.

[6] e.g. Gen. iii. 17 (J), vii. 11 (P); Lev. xviii. 18 (H); Deut. xxviii. 66; Judges xvi. 30; 2 Sam. i. 23; Job iii. 20; Ps. civ. 33; and so often.

ideal sense with reference to one's well-being, which is then normally understood and sometimes actually defined in terms of good health and material prosperity—including, of course, the implication of 'length of days'.[1] The conception of the 'Tree of Life', for example, even when shorn of its mythical associations,[2] carries with it the thought of more than mere longevity, as is clear from the contrasts afforded by its use in the book of Proverbs, e.g.:[3]

> Hope deferred maketh the heart sick,
>> But desire fulfilled is a tree of *life*.

> The tongue that healeth is a tree of *life*,
>> But distortion therewith is a shattering of spirit (רוּחַ).

The most striking example in this connexion, however, is that which is yielded by the Israelite sage's carefully qualified recommendation of Wisdom, i.e.:[4]

> Length of days is in her right hand;
>> In her left are riches and honour.
> Her ways are ways of pleasantness,
>> And all her paths are שָׁלוֹם (EVV. 'peace').
> She is a tree of *life* to those who grasp her,
>> And happy is each that holdeth her fast.

This close association of the term שָׁלוֹם (EVV. 'peace') with the term חַיִּים is also of special interest in view of the fact that it is now generally recognized that the former is somewhat inadequately rendered by the English word 'peace', and that it often enjoys the more active meaning which is conveyed by the term 'welfare'.[5] Nor is this the

---

[1] e.g. Deut. xxx. 20, xxxii. 47; Prov. iii. 2, 16–18 (as quoted later in the text); and (in the light of its context) Ps. xxi. 5 (EVV. 4).

[2] e.g. as preserved in Gen. ii. 9, iii. 22, 24 (all J). For the present writer's attitude to current theory concerning the mythical 'Tree of Life' and its survival in association with Israelite ideas of kingship, see *Myth, Ritual, and Kingship: Essays on the Theory and Practice of Kingship in the Ancient Near East and in Israel*, ed. S. H. Hooke (1958), pp. 231 f.

[3] Prov. xiii. 12, xv. 4: cf. xi. 30.   [4] Prov. iii. 16–18.

[5] The writer hopes to deal with √שלם, like √צדק, in what is planned as the immediate sequel to this monograph, i.e. *The Vitality of Society in the Thought of Ancient Israel*, as referred to above, p. 82, n. 1. Meantime see, for example, Pedersen, op. cit., pp. 243–61, E.T., pp. 311–35.

only passage in which these two words are brought into close association. The post-exilic prophet whose work is known to us as that of 'Malachi' also uses the same two terms to describe Yahweh's covenant with the Levites as implying 'life and well-being',[1] and again it is clear from the context that the reference is not to the mere continued existence of the Levitical order, but to its being in a continually flourishing condition; that is to say, the second term serves to define the first. An equally good example from another field is furnished by the psalmist when he says:[2]

> How precious is Thy devotion (חֶסֶד), O God,
>   When men take refuge in the shadow of Thy wings!
> They are regaled with the rich food of Thy house,
>   And Thou givest them to drink of Thy delightful stream;
> For with Thee is the spring of *life* (מְקוֹר חַיִּים);
>   It is through Thy light that we see light.

Here the immediate context, coupled with the psalmist's ultimate plea for deliverance from the oppressor, makes it clear that the reference is to an untroubled,[3] full, and prosperous life, which is picturesquely described as having its source in Yahweh.[4] Similarly, when the Deuteronomic writer insists that Israel's choice between fidelity and infidelity towards Yahweh resolves itself into a choice between 'life' and 'death', this is defined as involving on the one hand 'blessing' or 'good', and on the other the blight of 'curse' or 'evil';[5] and the context once more shows that the term חַיִּים implies not merely a long life but a full and prosperous one, i.e. involving fruitfulness of body, the

---

[1] Mal. ii. 5: cf. Prov. iii. 2.

[2] Ps. xxxvi. 8–10 (EVV. 7–9). The use of the term 'devotion' for the familiar Hebrew word חֶסֶד, as in the ensuing translation, was defended by the writer in a paper given before the Society for Old Testament Study at Cardiff in September 1946, and the text of this paper may now be found in the *Festschrift* referred to above, p. 86, n. 7, *ad fin.*

[3] Cf. Prov. xix. 23.

[4] In the light of this passage as a whole, therefore, it seems doubtful if we should emend the text in Job x. 12: cf., for example, Driver–Gray, I.C.C. (1921), *in loc.*

[5] Deut. xxx. 15–20.

fruitfulness of one's cattle, and the fruitfulness of the soil, together with rain in its season, outstanding success in commercial dealings with foreign nations, and a safe deliverance from every threat to the national well-being.[1] Accordingly (by way of a final example), when the psalmist defines the 'blessing' which Yahweh bestows on family unity as חַיִּים עַד־הָעוֹלָם (EVV. 'life for evermore'),[2] this implies more than the mere continuity of the kin-group. As the context clearly shows by its picturesque comparison with oil poured upon the head and dew descending upon Mount Hermon, the expression carries with it the thought of long-continued prosperity.[3] To sum up, in dealing with this whole realm of thought it is necessary to bear in mind that 'life' and 'death' are not always sharply disparate terms. Though poles apart in some respects, they are also used in a relative sense; for, ideally at least, 'life' is life in its fullness, and conversely any weakness in life is a form of 'death'.

All in all, therefore, we are now in a position to appreciate the wealth of meaning latent for the Israelite in the description of Yahweh as a (or the) 'Living God';[4] for there can be little doubt that it implies, not merely a contrast with false and therefore non-existent gods, but a vital activity on Yahweh's part as the 'Giver of Life', which may be seen to extend to the whole of creation,[5] and repeatedly makes itself felt on the plane of history.[6] Accordingly we

---

[1] Cf. Deut. xxviii. 1–14. [2] Ps. cxxxiii. 3.

[3] Cf. in the light of their context the following additional examples: Pss. xvi. 11, xxxiv. 13 (EVV. 12); Prov. iii. 22, iv. 22, 23, viii. 35, x. 11, 16, 17, xii. 28, xiii. 14, xiv. 27, 30, xv. 24, 31, xvi. 15, 22, xviii. 21, xix. 23, xxi. 21, xxii. 4. Note, too, the use of the term in Prov. xxvii. 27 (i.e. with the force of 'nourishment'), which may be compared with the use of the *Pi'ēl* as illustrated above, p. 99, n. 2.

[4] (a) אֵל חַי, Joshua iii. 10 (JE); Pss. xlii. 3 (EVV. 2), lxxxiv. 3 (EVV. 2); Hos. ii. 1 (EVV. i. 10): (b) אֱלֹהִים חַי, 2 Kings xix. 4, 16 (= Isa. xxxvii. 4, 17): (c) אֱלֹהִים חַיִּים, Deut. v. 23 (26); 1 Sam. xvii. 26, 36; Jer. x. 10, xxiii. 36. Cf. 2 Sam. xxii. 47 (= Ps. xviii. 47 (EVV. 46)).

[5] Cf., for example, Neh. ix. 6, as cited above, p. 99, n. 1.

[6] Cf., for example, Jer. xii. 16 f., xvi. 14 f., xxiii. 7 f. Note accordingly the force which lay for the believer behind the familiar words of the oath חַי יהוה,

can appreciate the better what it means for the prophet to speak of Yahweh as a 'Spring of Living Water' (מְקוֹר מַיִם חַיִּים),[1] and how important it is to be instructed in the 'Path of Life' (אֹרַח חַיִּים) or the 'Way of Life' (דֶּרֶךְ (הַ)חַיִּים),[2] and to have one's name written in the 'Book of Life' (סֵפֶר חַיִּים).[3] In fact, the important thing for every Israelite is that, as Abigail said of David, he should be 'bound up in the Bundle of Life (צְרוֹר הַחַיִּים)' with Yahweh his God.[4] The 'Land of Life' (אֶרֶץ (הַ)חַיִּים)[5] and the 'Light of Life' (אוֹר הַחַיִּים),[6] which afford such a strong contrast to the gloomy underworld of Sheol, are alike His;

&c.; and see further M. Greenberg, 'The Hebrew Oath Particle Ḥay/Ḥê', *J.B.L.* lxxvi (1957), pp. 34–39, for a useful, if controversial, discussion of the linguistic forms involved.

[1] Jer. ii. 13, xvii. 13. Cf. Ps. xxxvi. 10 (EVV. 9), as quoted above, p. 105; also Prov. x. 11, xiii. 14, xiv. 27, xvi. 22.

[2] (a) Ps. xvi. 11; Prov. v. 6, xv. 24: cf. Prov. ii. 19, x. 17: (b) Prov. vi. 23; Jer. xxi. 8. Cf. Ezek. xxxiii. 15 (חֻקּוֹת הַחַיִּים).

[3] Ps. lxix. 29 (EVV. 28): cf. R.V. See also p. 103, n. 5, with regard to the apparent ambiguity of the Hebrew, which may be held to denote the 'Book of the Living': cf. A.V., R.V. mgn., R.S.V., and see further, for example, Gunkel, H.K. (1926), *in loc.*, together with the following note. Cf. Exod. xxxii. 32 (J); Isa. iv. 3: also Pss. lvi. 9 (EVV. 8), cxxxix. 16; Mal. iii. 16.

[4] 1 Sam. xxv. 29. Note again what is for us an ambiguity in the Hebrew: i.e. cf. A.V. and R.V. with R.V. mgn. and R.S.V., and see the preceding note. Cf. now, also, the attractive explanation of this expression which is offered by O. Eissfeldt, *Der Beutel der Lebendigen: Alttestamentliche Erzählungs- und Dichtungsmotive im Lichte neuer Nuzi-Texte*, B.V.S.A.W.L. 105: 6 (1960), although I am not convinced that in Ps. lxix. 29 (EVV. 28) the parallelism requires one to think of 'the Book of the Living' rather than 'the Book of Life', and that, this being the case, one should think here of 'the Bundle of the Living' rather than 'the Bundle of Life' (op. cit., p. 22, n. 1: cf. Gunkel, loc. cit.). As is indicated above, p. 103 (i.e. where n. 5 is introduced), we are probably inclined to analyse too much in dealing with this term; in other words, we should probably recognize that for the Israelite it conveyed the thought of 'life' as manifested by 'the living'.

[5] Job xxviii. 13; Pss. xxvii. 13, lii. 7 (EVV. 5), cxlii. 6 (EVV. 5); Isa. xxxviii. 11, liii. 8; Jer. xi. 19; Ezek. xxvi. 20, xxxii. 23, 24, 25, 26, 27, 32: cf. Ps. cxvi. 9. The Hebrew offers the same ambiguity as that which is noticed in the two preceding notes, i.e. an alternative rendering is 'Land of the Living', as EVV., R.S.V.

[6] Job xxxiii. 30; Ps. lvi. 14 (EVV. 13). Note again the ambiguity of the Hebrew, which may be translated equally well by 'Light of the Living': cf. A.V. and R.V. with R.V. mgn. and R.S.V.

and in His power are the issues of 'life' and 'death'.[1] 'Am
I God (*or* a god) to cause to die and to make to live?', says
the king of Israel to Naaman the Syrian, when he seeks to
be healed of his leprosy;[2] and the background of thought is
that which appears in the words ascribed to Yahweh in the
Song of Moses:[3]

> See now that I, I am He,[4]
> And there is no god beside Me.
> 'Tis I who cause to die and make to live.
> If I have smitten, 'tis I must heal;
> And none can deliver out of My Hand.

Accordingly it is in this sense that we have to understand
the well-known words in the Prayer of Hannah:[5]

> Yahweh causeth to die and maketh to live,
> Bringeth down to Sheol and bringeth up.
> Yahweh maketh poor and maketh rich,
> Bringeth low, yea, raiseth high.

In short, the normal Israelite view, which dominates the
conception of man in the Old Testament, is that to be in
sickness of body or weakness of circumstance is to experience the disintegrating power of death, and to be brought by
Yahweh to the gates of Sheol; but to enjoy good health and

---

[1] Cf. Ps. lxviii. 21 (EVV. 20), as discussed in *Sacral Kingship in Ancient
Israel*, p. 73; Prov. iv. 23: and see further, for example, Pedersen, op. cit.,
pp. 353–86, E.T., pp. 453–96.

[2] 2 Kings v. 7: see above, p. 101.

[3] Deut. xxxii. 39.

[4] For the force of the 3rd personal pronoun in the emphatic declaration
הוּא אֲנִי אֲנִי (cf. Isa. xli. 4, xliii. 10, 13, xlvi. 4, xlviii. 12; also Ps. cii. 28
(EVV. 27)), see the data advanced in support of the suggested etymology
of the *tetragrammaton* by R. Otto, *Das Gefühl des Überweltlichen* (1932),
pp. 209 f., 326 f., quoting S. Mowinckel; M. Buber, *Königtum Gottes*,
2nd edit. enlarged (1936), pp. 235 f. (i.e. p. 84, n. 27), 3rd edit. enlarged
(1956), p. 185 (i.e. p. 69, n. 27), *Moses* (1947), pp. 49 f., citing B. Duhm in a
lecture (unpublished) at Göttingen; A. Vincent, *La Religion des Judéo-
Araméens d'Éléphantine* (1937), pp. 46 f.; J. A. Montgomery, 'The Hebrew
Divine Name and the Personal Pronoun *HŪ*', *J.B.L.* lxiii (1944), pp. 161–3;
and now Mowinckel's own formulation of the theory in 'The Name of the
God of Moses', *H.U.C.A.* xxxii (1961), pp. 121–33.

[5] 1 Sam. ii. 6 f.

material prosperity is to be allowed to walk with Him in fullness of life.[1]

[1] Perhaps the most striking parallel from the Assyro-Babylonian field is that afforded by the so-called 'Babylonian Job', lines 43–47, in which the author thus describes his fellow men:

> Like opening and closing their mood changeth.
> Should they be hungry, they are like a corpse;
> Should they be full, they rival their god.
> *When all is well, they speak of ascending to heaven;*
> *Should they be in trouble, they talk of descending to the underworld.*

For the text, see H. C. Rawlinson, *The Cuneiform Inscriptions of Western Asia*, iv, 2nd edit. rev. (1891), Plate 60*; also S. Langdon, *Babylonian Wisdom* (1923), Plate iv. For a transliteration and translation of this well-known passage, see Langdon, op. cit., p. 42: also P. (E.) Dhorme, *Choix de textes religieux assyro-babyloniens* (1907), pp. 376 f.; and (translation only) E. Ebeling, in *Altorientalische Texte zum Alten Testament*, ed. H. Gressmann, 2nd edit. rev. (1926), p. 275; and now R. H. Pfeiffer, in *Ancient Near Eastern Texts relating to the Old Testament*, ed. J. B. Pritchard, 2nd edit. rev. (1955), p. 435.

INDEX

(a) SUBJECTS

Where relevant page numbers apply to both text and footnotes.

Jehonadab, 83 n.
Jehoshaphat, 43.
Jehu, 15, 83 n.
Jeremiah, 8, 86.
Jerusalem, 5, 10 ff., 28 f., 31, 43, 88 n.
Jezreel, 15.
Joash, 59.
Job, 16 f., 29, 51, 67, 72, 73 n., 74, 94; Babylonian, 109 n.
Jonah, 5, 92 ff.
Jonathan, 17.
Joseph, 25, 27, 72.
Joshua, 56 n., 59, 96.
Joy, 12, 68 f., 76, 80. *See also* Exultation, Gladness.
Judgement, 31 f., 47, 55, 57 f.; moral, 45 ff., 47 f., 62 f. *See also* Discrimination.
Justice, 32, 46.

Kidney, 74 f., 87. *See also* Reins.
Kindliness, 40 f.
King, Kingship, 28 f., 34 f., 90, 97 f., 101, 104 n., 108.
Kin-group, 71 n., 101 n., 106.
Knee, 65.
Knowledge, 34, 46, 50, 78 f. *See also* Intellect, Intelligence.

Laban, 40, 53 n.
Levi, Levite, 60 n., 105.
Levirate marriage, 88 n.
Lex talionis, 71.
Life: conscious, 8, 18 f., 22; psychical, 8 n., 27, 30 ff., 45 ff., 50 ff., 67 ff., 74 ff., 87 f.; sentient, 9 ff.; as identifiable with blood, 8 f., 69; Book of, 107; Bundle of, 107; Land of, 94, 107; Light of, 107; Path of, 107; principle of, 8 f., 22, 69; Spring of, 87, 105 (cf. 107); Tree of, 104; Way of, 107; and order, 94 f. *See also* Animal life; Light; Vitality, degrees of.
Light: and life, 41 n., 94 f., 105.
Lip, 45 ff., 85 n.
Liver, 75 n.
Loathing, 12.
Loftiness, *see* Pride.
Loins, 73 f.
Longing, *see* Desire.
Lot, 20.
Love, 12, 17, 74.

Lowliness, *see* Humiliation, Humility.

Magic, 58 ff.; contagious, 3; homoeopathic or imitative, 3 n.
Malachi, 105.
Malice, 65.
Manasseh, 58.
Manslaughter, 71.
Memory, 78.
Mentality, prelogical, 1 n.
Messiah, 28 f. *See also* David.
Metaphor, 5 f., 53, 56 n., 64 n., 66 n., 67, 68 n., 85 n., 91 n., 92 n., 93 n. *See also* Figure of speech.
Metonymy, 49, 77. *See also* Figure of speech.
Midianite, 15 n.
Mind, 77 ff.; frame of, 31, 85.
Mischief, 46 f.
Mockery, 39, 55, 68.
Mood, 31, 40, 52 f., 64; oscillation in, 12, 26.
Moon, 53 n.
Moral standards, 82 ff.
Moses, 20, 35, 56 n., 59; Song of, 108.
Motive, 35 f., 73.
Mourning, 74 n.
Mouth, 5, 6 n., 45 ff., 65.
Murder, 71 f.

Naaman, 58, 96 n., 101, 108.
Nabal, 102 n.
Name: as an extension of the personality, 87 f. *See also* Yahweh.
Neck, 4 ff., 13 n., 22, 64 f., 93.
Nose, 45, 49.
Nostril, 6 f., 18 f., 28 f., 49 f.

Oath, 17 n., 18 n., 57 f., 106 n.
Obstinacy, 26, 35, 50, 64 f., 79 f.
Odour, 6 n., 24 n.
Offering, *see* Sacrifice.
Offspring: as an extension of the personality, 87 f.
Opportunity, 62.

Palate, 45 ff., 81 n.
Palm, *see* Hand.
Panic, 65.
Parallelism, 5 n., 6 n., 10 n., 16 f., 29, 38 f., 49 n., 51 f., 65 n., 69 n., 80 f., 83 n., 97 n., 98 n., 99 f.,

INDEX

(b) AUTHORS

Page numbers refer throughout to the footnotes.

INDEX

(c) SCRIPTURE REFERENCES

Where relevant page numbers apply to both text and footnotes.
All Old Testament references are to the Hebrew text.

INDEX

(d) SELECT HEBREW WORDS AND PHRASES

Where relevant page numbers apply to both text and footnotes.

PRINTED IN GREAT BRITAIN
AT THE UNIVERSITY PRESS, OXFORD
BY VIVIAN RIDLER
PRINTER TO THE UNIVERSITY